Peace in the Face of Loss is essential for anyone who's grieving or walking alongside a loved one in a difficult season. Loss knows no limits—Jill's story offers us hope and peace, and guides us back to the One who can comfort us best.

JOHN C. MAXWELL
New York Times bestselling author and leadership expert

I don't think I could oversell this book to you. Jill Kelly knows what she's talking about, and the message in *Peace in the Face of Loss* resonates deeply with me because I've known my share of pain and loss. And haven't we all? Haven't you? With a perfect blend of human frailty and God's strength, Jill shows us how to move forward in faith during the inevitable hard seasons of life. What a gift she's given us in this book!

CLAYTON KING
Senior pastor, NewSpring Church; founder and president, Crossroads Summer Camps and Clayton King Ministries

Jill Kelly has known heartache beyond what many can fathom. But in her pain, she has done something very few learn to do—she has discovered how to keep her heart connected to the Comforter, lifting her face to the presence of God to find the warmth of goodness in the midst of horrific storms. No matter what kind of pain you face, Jill knows how to shine a light in the darkness, leading others to freedom and offering clarity to bring hope and healing.

CHRISTA BLACK GIFFORD
Songwriter, speaker, and author of *Heart Made Whole*

PEACE
IN THE FACE OF
LOSS

JILL KELLY

TYNDALE
MOMENTUM™

The nonfiction imprint of
Tyndale House Publishers, Inc.

Visit Tyndale online at www.tyndale.com.

Visit Tyndale Momentum online at www.tyndalemomentum.com.

Visit the author at jillk.org.

TYNDALE, *Tyndale Momentum*, and Tyndale's quill logo are registered trademarks of Tyndale House Publishers, Inc. The Tyndale Momentum logo is a trademark of Tyndale House Publishers, Inc. Tyndale Momentum is the nonfiction imprint of Tyndale House Publishers, Inc., Carol Stream, Illinois.

Peace in the Face of Loss

Edited by Karin Stock Buursma

Designed by Eva Winters

Published in association with The Christopher Ferebee Agency, www.christopherferebee.com.

All Scripture quotations, unless otherwise indicated, are taken from the Holy Bible, *New International Version,*® *NIV.*® Copyright © 1973, 1978, 1984, 2011 by Biblica, Inc.® (Some quotations may be from the earlier NIV edition, copyright © 1984.) Used by permission. All rights reserved worldwide.

Scripture quotations marked ESV are taken from *The Holy Bible*, English Standard Version® (ESV®), copyright © 2001 by Crossway, a publishing ministry of Good News Publishers. Used by permission. All rights reserved.

Scripture quotations marked KJV are taken from the *Holy Bible*, King James Version.

Scripture quotations marked *The Message* are taken from *THE MESSAGE* by Eugene H. Peterson, copyright © 1993, 1994, 1995, 1996, 2000, 2001, 2002. Used by permission of NavPress Publishing Group. All rights reserved.

Scripture quotations marked NASB are taken from the New American Standard Bible,® copyright © 1960, 1962, 1963, 1968, 1971, 1972, 1973, 1975, 1977, 1995 by The Lockman Foundation. Used by permission.

Scripture quotations marked NKJV are taken from the New King James Version,® copyright © 1982 by Thomas Nelson, Inc. Used by permission. All rights reserved.

Scripture quotations marked NLT are taken from the *Holy Bible*, New Living Translation, copyright © 1996, 2004, 2015 by Tyndale House Foundation. Used by permission of Tyndale House Publishers, Inc., Carol Stream, Illinois 60188. All rights reserved.

Out of respect for their privacy, the names and identifying details of some people in this book have been changed.

For information about special discounts for bulk purchases, please contact Tyndale House Publishers at csresponse@tyndale.com or call 800-323-9400.

ISBN 978-1-4964-2136-4

Printed in China

23	22	21	20	19	18	17
7	6	5	4	3	2	1

To my son, Hunter.

Your legacy of love continues to change lives, including mine.

I love you!

Mostly it is loss which teaches us about the worth of things.

ARTHUR SCHOPENHAUER

A NOTE FROM THE AUTHOR

MORE THAN LIKELY, you have this book in your hands because either you or someone you know and love has suffered loss. You may have lost a child or a sibling, a spouse or a parent. Perhaps you're dealing with infertility, infidelity, or abuse, or you're mourning the loss of a relationship, a job, or a career path you were certain of. You may be grieving over a life that is far from what you expected it to be. Whatever the circumstances that may have converged to bring you to this unwelcome place, you are not on the outside looking in—you're hurting. At this point, you don't know what to say or do. Words fall short and your prayers seem hollow. Tears come unexpectedly and often, and you never thought it was possible to weep so much.

Perhaps you're desperate for hope and healing but cannot seem to muster up either one despite your best efforts. First and foremost, I want you to know that although we've never met and probably never will this side of heaven, I care about you. And although I might not have endured the unique losses you have or suffered the pain you've experienced, I long for the same peace and healing that you crave.

You might assume that the author of a book like this would

have a PhD in Coping with Loss. If not a degree, then certainly a deep well with some serious life experiences to draw from in order to back up the claims made. If I'm pregnant with my firstborn, I'm not searching the web for parenting advice written by someone who has never raised children. Are you tracking with me? You don't seek counsel from someone who has never experienced what you need advice about.

Let's be frank: If someone has never languished in the bottom of a pit and found her way back to the top, what makes her think she can encourage, guide, or bring hope to someone who's in the pit right now?

There's no question that I have been in the bottom of the pit, starting with my son Hunter's diagnosis of a terminal disease when he was just four months old and continuing past his death at the age of eight and a half. So here's my confession: I'm not all the way out of the pit yet.

When I was asked to write this devotional, I was humbled and grateful. It's one thing to have a book idea, draft a proposal, and then find a publisher that buys into what you think everyone needs to read. It's an even rarer honor and privilege to have a publisher approach you to write on a topic that they feel you can speak about to readers in a meaningful way. Initially, I believed that my experiences of loss would allow me to confidently communicate what I have learned and the peace I have experienced as a result.

But that's not entirely the case.

No, what God revealed to me in the midst of writing this book was different from what I had envisioned. As I reflected on my profound and painful losses, I expected to remember the pain and to a certain degree feel it all over again, but I assumed that this time it wouldn't be as raw and fresh because the emotional bleeding had stopped and the wound had healed. But instead, as I reflected and remembered, I realized that some of the residual pain is still there and I don't always have the peace I've been asked to write about.

I don't have all the answers. Therefore, I'm not writing this book because I have successfully completed my grieving process and now live in perfect peace. Instead, through my journey of loss, I have discovered that the people who have helped me the most are those who have walked beside me, cried with me, and pointed me back to God. That is exactly what I hope to do for you. Because while finding peace in the midst of heartbreak and loss sounds impossible, Scripture tells us that "with God all things are possible" (Matthew 19:26).

While encouraging words might carry us through a day or two, what we really crave is peace that surpasses all understanding—the kind of perfect peace that's rock solid, sustaining, and uplifting, no matter what happens around us or within us. I want what is impossible for me to obtain in and of my own strength.

If that's what you desire, I invite you to join me as we, together, seek and find peace through and from the Author and Prince of Peace. He is our starting point because, simply put, we cannot know true healing, abiding hope, joy, and peace unless we know Him. Everything—and I mean *everything*—we need in this moment and for the rest of our days upon this earth is found in Christ.

Maybe that is exactly what you didn't want to hear. At this point in your life, you may feel that God has let you down, and as a result you're done with faith and all that goes along with it. If that's you, please, don't put this book down. Don't walk away. God is capable of handling whatever you throw at Him; nothing you do or don't do will negatively impact His outrageous love for you. He knows you better than you know yourself, and He's big enough to handle all your anger, rejection, and bitterness.

He's not finished with you yet. Will you consider giving Him another chance, another opportunity to meet you right where you are in the midst of your loss? We are all a work in progress. We need Him and each other, so let's do this together. Let's trust God, one day at a time, one prayer at a time, all in His perfect timing.

In this book you will find forty devotions that touch on different aspects of loss. You'll learn a lot about my story but will hear from some other people as well. Each devotion begins with a Bible verse or quote and ends with a "path to peace" statement that summarizes the chapter and conveys a word of truth for you to ponder and apply to your life. You'll also find Scripture in each chapter to encourage you as you continue your journey through loss.

Let's choose to trust God one devotion at a time.

And when we both reach the last line of this book, I believe we will be different people than we were when we first started this journey. I'm praying for you and trusting God to bring the life-changing peace to your life that only He can provide.

With hope . . . and peace,
Jill

*Many are the plans in a person's heart, but it is
the LORD's purpose that prevails.*

PROVERBS 19:21

HE WAS THE PROTÉGÉ SON. A chip off the old block, the heir to a celebrated football legacy—and the culmination of a father's hopes and dreams. Before our only son, Hunter, was born, his life had been scripted, written upon his father's heart like a playbook for the next generation. Like father, like son; he would grow up with the spiritual grit to be a courageous, honorable, and determined young man. He would be gifted—an all-star athlete (a quarterback, of course) and a tough competitor who would wear the number twelve just like his dad. He would work hard, doing more than what was expected of him and never giving up despite the setbacks that would come his way.

He would get up before the crack of dawn to go fishing

and hunting with his dad. Their relationship would be the envy of every father and son as he would grow in wisdom and pay close attention to each piece of advice he was given, jumping at every chance to make the Kelly family proud. These were just some of the scenes we had already written into the life script for Hunter James Kelly.

I will never forget the joy and pride radiating from my husband, Jim's, face when our son was born. I had found out during a routine sonogram that we were having a boy and decided that I would surprise Jim rather than tell him before the baby was born. My water broke on Jim's birthday—Valentine's Day, February 14, 1997. The son Jim had always wanted was born on his birthday, signaling a perfect beginning to a perfect story. Or so we thought . . .

Shortly after we brought Hunter home from the hospital, he became very irritable and started to have difficulty eating. More serious issues surfaced, leading us through a whirlwind of doctors' visits that resulted in a barrage of tests to try to determine exactly what was wrong. Finally, when Hunter was four months old, a neurologist diagnosed him with a fatal genetic disease called Krabbe leukodystrophy. (If you are interested in learning more about Hunter's incredible life, please visit the Hunter's Hope Foundation website at http://www.huntershope.org.)

Words are pathetically powerless to describe the devastation you feel when you're told that your child will most likely not live to see his second birthday. It is impossible to express the avalanche of anguish that buries you when the doctor explains that there is no cure or treatment for the disease that is killing your infant son.

In an instant, any vestige of faith you have is overwhelmed by sheer dread. Swallowed by the darkness of a disease diagnosis, you feel powerless and helpless, devastated and desperate for hope.

Hunter never experienced or accomplished any of the things his father had dreamed he would. He never threw a pass into the end zone for the winning touchdown. He never sat in a ground blind while turkey hunting with his dad or did any of the fun, simple things that young, healthy, growing boys do. And although he lived far beyond what the doctors had predicted, Hunter's life was filled with suffering.

Yet, in the midst of his suffering—the suffering that went against all the plans we had for our son's life—we began to understand that God had a greater purpose for Hunter's life and for our family. We saw glimpses of it as our girls developed remarkable compassion from loving their brother and as we experienced the solidarity and love of "Team Hunter"—our amazing team of family, friends, medical staff, and therapists who helped with the daily care of our boy. We saw a piece of it through the lives touched by the Hunter's Hope Foundation and most of all as we loved Hunter himself. It took time and a tremendous amount of trust and tears, but we learned to let go of our plans in order to grab hold of God's hand. Rather than continue to try to write our own script the way we thought it should be written, we learned to trust God, the Giver of life and Author of every story.

Can we get real with each other right now? You and I both want life to be fair. We want our lives to go a certain way—our way. We think the American Dream is a reasonable goal, so we spend ourselves in its pursuit. We strive to obtain what we want but then find ourselves empty and longing for more. We think we know what is best when in reality it's impossible to see the big picture from our vantage point.

And when life doesn't pan out or conform to our preconceived notions, or when it falls short of our plans and hands us a loss we didn't expect—the fallout is often devastating.

If you're reading this book, you have experienced loss—and I know that loss can feel like your dreams have been crushed and life is a mess. But what if what you need is the exact opposite of what you think you need? What if the very thing that causes you the greatest pain ends up being the greatest blessing?

The Bible reminds us that God's plans are far greater than our own:

> He is the Rock, his works are perfect,
>   and all his ways are just.
> A faithful God who does no wrong,
>   upright and just is he.

DEUTERONOMY 32:4

When we hold on to the truth that God's ways are perfect, it can change the way we react to loss. We can pray instead of plan. We can trust God and accept what is instead of trying so hard to change everything and everyone. We can even entertain the radical idea that the very loss we're going through right now might be the catalyst to immeasurable blessing. We can let go and let God do what only He can do.

Peace in the face of loss comes when we let go of our plans and **embrace God's perfect purposes**.

2

In him all things were created: things in heaven and on earth, visible and invisible, whether thrones or powers or rulers or authorities; all things have been created through him and for him. He is before all things, and in him all things hold together.

COLOSSIANS 1:16-17

I'LL BE HONEST WITH YOU: After watching my son suffer for eight and a half years, then struggling through his death and the suffocating grief and depression that followed, I felt like both shoes had dropped at the same time. I assumed that I had fulfilled my life quota of tears and heartbreak. No one should have to bury a child, right? But people do, and I did. That experience wrecked me. I am not the same person I was before I endured that loss—nor should I be. If you have experienced the death of a child, you know what I'm talking about. You will never be the same. Ever.

But the other shoe actually dropped when my husband, Jim, was diagnosed with oral cancer—known medically as squamous cell carcinoma of the upper jaw. He would go on to have his upper left jaw surgically removed. Upon full recovery and healing, a clean scan revealed the results we had all been praying for: "no cancer." Then, almost a year after his surgery, the cancer returned with a vengeance, requiring the most aggressive chemotherapy and radiation regimen. Even now as I type this, I'm waiting to hear the results of his most recent MRI and other scans. He's been cancer-free for close to two years now (praise God!), but once you've had cancer, these types of scans become routine. Unfortunately, Jim's been in a lot of pain lately, more than usual, so there's greater concern and fear.

But I'm not the only one who seems to have more than my quota of sorrow. There's my dear friend Nicole. To this very day, I still wrestle with God because of her death. She was a momma to twin boys, Trevor and Tyler, and we met because Trevor has the same disease that my son, Hunter, had. Nicole was the strong Wonder Woman type. She was also fun, gracious, kind, and gentle—but when it came to taking care of her boys, especially Trevor, she was a force to be reckoned with. I had (and still have) tremendous admiration, love, and respect for her.

I got word one day from a mutual friend that Nicole had been diagnosed with breast cancer. I was shocked; we all were. Isn't taking care of a terminally ill child enough heartbreak to bear? Nicole fought hard and long, but eventually the cancer spread. My first thought after I heard that Nicole died was *Who's going to take care of Trevor?* Yes, Nicole's husband is an amazing and capable father, but there's nothing like a mother's care. Why didn't God heal Hunter and Nicole?

It's not only diseases that cause us to ask *Why?* We ask

when we hear about another mass shooting or terrorist attack, or when we watch or read the news about another child abuse case or fatal car accident. Why does God let this happen?

If there ever was a person whom we might assume had the right to ask why, it was Job. My uncle Mark introduced me to Job soon after we found out that Hunter was dying. Mark would come over to the house often, and every time he came he brought his Bible, his smile, and so much Jesus joy that it was contagious. He read me the story of Job, which is exactly what I needed to hear during that season in my life. (It's still one of my favorites.)

The book of Job is difficult to read, even for the seasoned Bible student. Job's story is shocking and heartbreaking because it's a true story about a man suffering more loss than anyone I have ever met. First, Job lost his wealth. He was the Bill Gates of his day, the wealthiest man around, and in an instant he lost everything—oxen, donkeys, sheep, servants, camels. All of it.

The losses didn't end there. Soon after Job received word that his possessions had been taken,

> yet another messenger came and said, "Your sons and daughters were feasting and drinking wine at the oldest brother's house, when suddenly a mighty wind swept in from the desert and struck the four corners of the house. It collapsed on them and they are dead, and I am the only one who has escaped to tell you!"
> JOB 1:18-19

All his sons and daughters died. All of them. Not one was spared. Can you even imagine? I don't know about you, but in that moment, I would have wished I had died with the children. How do you survive?

Job's response after hearing about the death of his children wrecks me even more:

> At this, Job got up and tore his robe and shaved his head. Then he fell to the ground in worship and said:
>
> "Naked I came from my mother's womb,
>   and naked I will depart.
> The LORD gave and the LORD has taken away;
>   may the name of the LORD be praised."
>
> JOB 1:20-21

As if Job hadn't encountered enough pain, after the loss of his children he continued to suffer physically through painful sores from the bottom of his feet to the top of his head. Job lost his wealth, his health, and his children.

When Job finally broke and questioned God, it wasn't because of his losses but because of his inability to understand *why* God would allow him to suffer the way he did. And in the end, God never sat down with Job and explained why. Instead of giving Job answers, God asked Job a flurry of questions, starting with "Where were you when I laid the earth's foundation?" (Job 38:4). God revealed more of

Himself—His majesty, His sovereignty, His power, His care for creation—and that was more than enough for Job.

If you understood why you suffered the losses you have, would it take away the loss itself? No. Would your heart be free of pain? No, because knowledge alone doesn't heal. Your heart would still ache. Though it may be hard to grasp, what healed Job's anguish is what heals ours: more of God. In the end, what mends our brokenness is love, which is simply more of God, since the Bible proclaims that "God is love" (1 John 4:8).

Broken hearts are not mended by theology, church, friends, family, time, or even answers to the *why* of our suffering and losses. Hearts are made whole by love—because real, unconditional love never fails. And it's this kind of love alone that enables us to trust a Creator who does not explain Himself to His creation. Because if we know He loves us, it's enough that He knows the answers.

Peace in the face of loss comes when we boldly ask God the hard "why" questions and **humbly trust Him with the answers**.

3

Don't stand in pious judgment
Of the bonds I must untie,
Don't tell me how to suffer,
And don't tell me how to cry.

J. HENDEL

BEFORE I BECAME A CHRISTIAN, she was the one who had relentlessly prayed for me and my family. She not only prayed but also put action to her prayers with a heart full of faith that reached into our lives in multiple ways. Because of her selfless giving, compassion, and gentle spirit, I knew she was different. And yet until I understood what that difference was, I thought she was just really nice and radically "religious."

She talked about Jesus all the time and had an unbridled joy that was contagious. I felt an overwhelming sense of peace whenever I was around her, so spending time together was always a blessing. Since she lived a few houses down from us in the cul-de-sac, if we needed a couple of eggs, we'd call her and within minutes she would be at the door with a dozen. The neighborhood kids knew that her doors were always open, and youth groups met in her basement on a weekly basis for years. If I had a "God question," she was the first person I would ask, and the first Bible study I ever participated in was held in her living room. She loved our family unconditionally even though she knew not just the good, but the bad and the ugly as well. Faithful and trustworthy, she was and still is one of my closest friends.

Still, I will never forget her words that day. It was a few months after Hunter went to heaven, during the darkest and most difficult days of my grief journey. She knew I was having a rough day and needed a praying friend, so she came. After we had prayed, we walked toward the front door, and before she left she turned toward me and casually said, "Maybe you should consider taking down some of Hunter's pictures. You wouldn't want to make an idol or shrine out of them."

Shocked and *confused* are the only words that accurately describe how I felt in that moment. Shocked that she said those words. Confused because the pictures she was referring to had always been there—we hadn't added any new ones. My confusion quickly turned to resentment. I remember thinking, *Wait a minute, is she telling me how to grieve, suggesting there's a better way? She knows nothing of the road I'm traveling; it's the one less traveled, and it seems to be growing longer and harder every day.*

I wish I could tell you that the sting of her words subsided shortly after they were spoken. But I was hurt, angry, and sad for a long time. Long enough for those raw emotions to burrow deep into my heart and ripen into bitterness and anger. Eventually, as is often the case, those deep-seated emotions began to bear the ugly fruit of unforgiveness. And although we were neighbors and sisters in Christ, as a result of my pain a chasm formed between us, causing me to try to avoid her as often as possible.

Whenever we crossed paths, these words rolled through my mind: "You're idolizing Hunter." She never said that, but that's exactly how it played, over and over like a broken record. I often wondered if she was right and contemplated taking down some of our family pictures. The more time that went by, however, the more frustrated and upset I grew. Of course, in retrospect I certainly could have handled the situation better, with a more mature, godlier attitude—but I was the one grieving. And in the midst of grief, we don't always "handle it better," because sometimes grief has a way of "handling" us.

Over time and as I continued to heal, God in His mercy and love revealed the unforgiveness I had allowed to fester in my heart. He began to replace the lies that my friend's words had spoken over me with the truth of His unconditional, perfect love. He also reminded me of how much I had been forgiven and what His Son did to provide a way for me to receive forgiveness. Because I have been forgiven, He asks me to extend that same grace and mercy to others, as Colossians 3:13 says:

Bear with each other and forgive one another if any of you has a grievance against someone. Forgive as the Lord forgave you.

The more I focused on His grace, the more I realized what I could not grasp the moment my dear friend spoke those words: She could not know or understand my pain . . . but God does.

He alone knows the depths of our hearts and the pain we endure. He sees the unseen and hears the unspoken. He knows everything. I had expected my beloved friend to know what she could not know, to feel what she could not feel, and to understand what only God could understand perfectly and completely. We all have a tendency to do this, don't we? We *expect* from people what only God can deliver.

But here's the thing. The beauty in all of this is that when our expectations are not met through people, it causes us to look elsewhere for satisfaction. And God knows that when we get to the end of searching for satisfaction, hope, and peace in all the wrong places and faces—He's still there. He's there ready and willing to fulfill the expectations that only He could fulfill from the start.

It took a long time for me to let my treasured friend off the hook. I thought I had forgiven her, but then resentment would rear its ugly head and I would have to forgive again. But it did come eventually, and a tremendous sense of relief, peace, and freedom came along with it. Even now, as I type this, God is revealing more to me. There are more people I need to forgive, including myself.

Have you been hurt by others who said the wrong thing or failed to understand your grief? Whom do you need to forgive? I know it's not easy, but at the very least I hope you will take the time to pray. Talk to God. Be honest with Him. Because at the end of the day, unforgiveness hurts you more than it does anyone else.

> He does not treat us as our sins deserve
> or repay us according to our iniquities.
> For as high as the heavens are above the earth,
> so great is his love for those who fear him;
> as far as the east is from the west,
> so far has he removed our transgressions from us.
>
> PSALM 103:10-12

> Be kind and compassionate to one another, forgiving each other, just as in Christ God forgave you.
>
> EPHESIANS 4:32

Peace in the face of loss comes when we **choose to forgive those who have hurt us**.

4

No one ever told me that grief felt so like fear.

C. S. LEWIS, *A GRIEF OBSERVED*

IT WAS JUST EIGHT MONTHS after my eight-year-old son, Hunter, had gone to heaven, and it seemed as though time had evaporated. Up until that morning I had believed that I was adjusting to his absence fairly well—if there is such a thing as adjusting when your heart has been torn from your soul.

And although sleep was elusive, I still rose early every morning and pasted on the best smile I could muster. Concern for our two daughters, Erin and Camryn, and their wounded hearts easily eclipsed my own heartbreak, so I focused on their healing above my own.

For the good of everyone under our roof, I kept moving and living. I stayed busy doing everything that needed to be done. From the mundane routine of keeping house to more complicated projects, I stayed in motion scrubbing, washing, and dusting—anything that kept me doing and doing because *being* was just too hard.

So I kept busy. And as draining as it all was given the emotional fallout I was wading through, I continued to press on. I was living—at times I barely endured and at times I gloriously triumphed, but I was moving forward and surviving the worst possible thing that a parent could ever experience. But then it happened . . .

When I went to bed one night, everything seemed as normal as it could be given the circumstances. However, the following morning, I didn't wake up to the light of day but to thick, debilitating darkness.

I'd heard stories about depression but never dreamed that I would find myself in the midst of it. Sounds of life and expressions of hope were as muffled and vague as if everything were underwater. Food lost its flavor, so eating was meaningless. And it was not only dark, it was forbidding. The only thing I can liken it to is a nightmare—the kind that scares you half to death, sticks with you, and takes months to shake.

It was far worse than a nightmare, though, because it was real and I was wide awake. During this darkness, simple things were not so simple anymore. I wanted to drive but couldn't. When I got behind the wheel, the air in the car became so thick that simply taking a breath became an unnerving challenge. Visions of hitting other cars or smashing into guardrails eventually led me from the driver's side to the passenger's seat. And that was just the beginning.

I echoed David's anguish of heart and his words in Psalm 13:1-2:

> How long, LORD? Will you forget me forever?
>> How long will you hide your face
>>> from me?
> How long must I wrestle with my thoughts
>> and day after day have sorrow in
>>> my heart?

I had heard women share about this kind of darkness and fear over the years, usually after I'd spoken at an event. I'd listen to their desperate, agonizing stories . . . stories punctuated by rivers of tears that streamed from swollen eyes that had seen far too much sorrow.

Countless broken women would tell me of unspeakable loss, of the deaths they had endured. They would share details and pictures of their beautiful children, their countenances draped with a pain that words cannot adequately describe. And their eyes . . .

Their eyes peered wearily into a distant place—a place I had never been. As they spoke, it was as if their words were simply tears that could be heard. They would elaborate on anxiety and depression, speaking of darkness and dreadful things I had never experienced and prayed I never would. Hunter was still alive at the time, so I could not fully understand their pain, nor was I equipped to bear their burdens along with my own. These grieving women were not looking for an answer to their pain, although sometimes (and I hate to admit this) I did my best to give one. They were not looking for me to do anything but listen . . . so that's mostly what I tried to do.

From all that I had heard from these women, and all I understood about God, I knew that I would not be able to endure this darkness in and of my own strength. I was desperate. I needed prayer and prayer warriors, and the first person to come to the rescue was my mother.

She had come alongside me in every aspect of Hunter's care. We did it together, and this passage through the valley of the shadow of death was no different. She wept with me, held me, and listened as I tried desperately to find my way again. She drove when I no longer could, and she talked to the doctors when all I could do was cry. And though I don't remember anything she said during those dark days that drifted into months, I do remember that she was there for me.

Hers, however, was not the only comfort I received from God as I fumbled through the emotional and spiritual wilderness. My heart was strengthened by the voices of those women who had shared their broken, weary hearts with me. Their stories echoed across the years, and the memory of their tears brought me comfort. What I could not fully understand before, I now knew firsthand.

God, in His sovereignty, continues to use the very heart-break and loss that could have destroyed me. He uses that very pain—and the comfort I received in the midst of it—to reach out into the pain of others. The tears of sorrow that overwhelmed me have become building blocks of hope that have helped me lead others out of their own valley of the shadow of death.

And I believe God will do the same with your pain.

No matter what type of loss you are in the midst of right now, it is no match for the power and love of God. His perfect peace and comfort are available for you. And even if the darkness and fear are great, God is greater still. He is your comfort, and He has strategically placed people in your life who will stand in the gap and pray with you until you get through this season. You are not alone.

And on the other side of the dark valley, you will stand back and watch in awe as God begins to use the very heart-break and loss you were convinced would destroy *you* to encourage and comfort others.

As Paul wrote so eloquently in 2 Corinthians 1:3-4,

Praise be to the God and Father of our Lord Jesus Christ, the Father of compassion and the God of all comfort, who comforts us in all our troubles, so that we can comfort those in any trouble with the comfort we ourselves receive from God.

Peace in the face of loss comes when we
receive comfort from God and then choose
to extend that comfort to others.

5

*Live each and every day as if it were your last—
because one day you'll be right.*

BOB MOAWAD

I GUESS IT'S FAIR to say that often when we hear the words *loss* or *lost*, our thoughts immediately drift to death. We hear the words in that context far more often than we want to—"He lost a child" or "She lost her mom." And even though few things are more painful, occasionally a mixed blessing is woven into the tapestry of this meaning of loss—a blessing that brings a measure of peace where it is not easily found. Such was the case for my friend Rick.

He had gone down south to spend Father's Day with his dad, whom he saw just once or twice a year. It was a big deal because his dad had been battling a host of medical problems for several years—problems that included a rare blood disorder, heart issues, strokes, and finally cancer. To say it had been a tough few years would be a gross understatement. Yet the man was absolutely resolute, soldiering on regardless of what life threw at him.

My friend drove down sixteen hours straight from New York State, arriving about 9 p.m. the Friday before Father's Day. As he emerged from the car, the familiar sights, sounds, and scents of the South embraced him, and his parents' embraces followed right behind. It was a joyous reunion, but it didn't take Rick long to see that his father was really struggling. Something wasn't right. After some discussion, his father agreed to go to the hospital the following morning if he didn't feel better. For the moment, it was late and his dad just wanted to get to bed, so that was the plan.

It was a reasonable plan. But like all plans, it was subject to change. Plans change because life changes, and the truth is, the only two things that don't change in this world are change and God.

Rick was just finishing getting ready for the day at about 7 a.m. when his mother appeared at his bedroom door with a fearful, shocked look on her face. She blurted out, "Go look upstairs in the bathroom!" An uneasy feeling crawled up his spine as he climbed the stairs, and when he reached the bathroom he found his father's body. His dad must have gotten up during the night, in trouble, and gone into the bathroom to try to ride it out. He'd leaned against the wall and then peacefully slid down into the arms of eternity.

The next couple of hours were chaotic, punctuated by a plethora of phone calls, the ambulance, the funeral director, friends, rivers of tears, and a whole lot of painful decisions.

And then Rick and his mother were alone again—without his father.

In the midst of it all, Rick felt a profound and overriding comfort that he had been home when the unthinkable happened. What were the odds that this tragic turn of events would unfold during his once-a-year visit? As it played out, he was able to see his father one last time. He was able to comfort his mother during one of the worst experiences of her life. He was able to offer advice and support, and he could help move a very painful set of circumstances forward.

Rick could have been bitter, depressed, and angry at the Lord for taking his dad. Instead he witnessed the hand of God orchestrate peace and healing in the midst of sudden heartbreak and loss. He understood that so many things had gone remarkably right that could have gone wrong, and among them was the blessing that his mother did not have to weather the initial heartbreak of this storm alone.

Don't get me wrong; none of this was easy. Rick sat there looking at the Father's Day gift he had brought with him, the one his dad never opened, and he pondered not just the unforeseen future but also the past—from his childhood to that morning. His time with his dad was over; that was all they got. And even though he wanted more, Rick had to make peace with an abrupt ending.

However, because he wholeheartedly believed that God led him to be there at the right time, he was able to summon the courage to carry on with an appreciative heart instead of a hard one. With peace in his soul, he reflected on all that his dad meant to him as he penned the obituary. He was able to begin the grieving process in a healthy way.

Rick understood that his dad's death was not a surprise to God; it came in God's perfect timing. As Psalm 139:15-16 says,

> My frame was not hidden from you
> > when I was made in the secret place,
> > when I was woven together in the depths
> > > of the earth.
> Your eyes saw my unformed body;
> > all the days ordained for me were written
> > > in your book
> > before one of them came to be.

Because he understood this, Rick found a way to focus on hope instead of despair, joy rather than sorrow, and appreciation as opposed to bitterness and anger. What he gained was peace in the midst of a heartbreaking loss that every child must one day face.

🍃 🍃 🍃

Do you believe that you can experience peace too? Do you believe that it's possible to hope again despite what you've had to endure? It's okay if your answer to the last few questions is an emphatic *no*. But let me suggest this. What if you asked God to help you believe that in and through Him, peace, joy, and hope are possible? What if in the midst of your pain and grief you asked God to show you what can only be seen through His grace?

No matter what kinds of losses we've experienced, most of us face moments when we have to choose what our perspectives will be. We can choose bitterness and anger toward God because of what has happened to us—and most of us will choose that sometimes. We see from the Psalms that even King David railed against God during the darkest moments of his suffering. But then we can step back and choose to remember that God is God and He's good. We can look for evidence of His hand in the details of our circumstances— because we are sure to find it. He does not leave us comfortless; He does not keep His grace from us. His blessings are there if we ask for His help to see them.

> Peace in the face of loss can be experienced when we **look for God's hand** in the midst of our brokenness.

6

Teach us to number our days aright,
that we may gain a heart of wisdom.

PSALM 90:12

"LIFE IS SHORT," she sighed as my daughter Erin and I leaned in to listen.

We had just left the house to go for a walk, and as we reached the end of the driveway, our neighbor Netka walked to the road to greet us. She and her husband live directly across the street from us in a beautiful white brick home surrounded by a shiny black wrought-iron fence. I'm not certain of their ages, but I would say they are both in their late seventies. Netka and Chris are from Macedonia and have accents as strong as their love and work ethic.

When we moved into our home, Netka and Chris were the first to welcome us. Humble, gracious, and down to earth, Netka would often bring us a basket full of fruit and vegetables from her garden. If we were out walking, she would wave us over so she could treat us to a fresh lemon from her tree or homemade bread hot from the oven.

She and Chris worked their land, taking great pride in the fruit of their labors as they cultivated the blessings God had given them. In fact, I'm pretty sure it was Netka's garden that inspired Jim to plant the one we now have in our backyard. These people are the salt-of-the-earth type—the kind of humble, honest folk you love spending time with because you know their priorities are solid and they genuinely care about you.

Before that day when Erin and I stopped to visit with Netka, it had seemed like years since we talked with each other. Time has a way of going by so fast that we don't even realize it until moments like this one. When we approached Netka, she looked tired, careworn, and sad. She had been working on the flower beds near the iron-gated entrance to her home when she saw us.

The first thing I did was hug her, despite the dirt she was blanketed with and the mud-caked garden trowel she clutched in her hand. Initially there was a lot of small talk between the three of us. She asked about Jim and how he was feeling, and then we talked about what the girls were up to for the summer. And even though she was able to carry on a conversation with a smile, I knew something was wrong. After we had shared all the latest happenings in the Kelly household, I asked Netka how she was doing.

It seems like such a simple question, doesn't it? And yet it's not simple at all, at least not for those walking through loss, heartbreak, and grief. I can't even begin to count how many times I have been asked, "How's Jim doing?" I'm grateful that people care and take the time to ask, but sometimes that simple question can bring a flood of emotions and tears. Honestly, even though Jim might be doing just fine when I am asked, that doesn't mean that our circumstances are easy or that he's not still struggling. Life is hard and the daily siege is real, assailing us on so many levels from emotional to physical to spiritual.

Netka went on to share how she had been in mourning for the last three years. Yes, three years. Her beloved brother had died, and despite her best efforts at healthy grieving, she was struggling, overwhelmed by sorrow, heartbreak, and loss. She had stopped doing what she had always done: gardening, tending to her flowers and trees, and going to church. It was almost as if she were trying to tell us that she had not left the house until that very moment when we stopped to talk. My heart hurt for her and with her. At the end of our conversation, there was a brief, awkward silence. Then Netka looked from me to Erin and sighed, "Life is short. Enjoy the time you have together while you still have it." We hugged good-bye, and then Erin and I turned to walk away while Netka slowly meandered back to her flower garden.

* * *

"Life is short." It may sound like a one-size-fits-all cliché, but it's the most common response to a death in the family, divorce, or a tragic event on the evening news, because it's true. Life is short, period. There are no exceptions. We all have a limited number of heartbeats. We don't have to live long to know this; we merely have to open the eyes of our hearts and step outside ourselves. We live in a fading world filled with very few days, no matter how many years we have.

The poet David wrote eloquently about our transient lives, comparing humans to grass and wildflowers:

> The LORD is like a father to his children,
>   tender and compassionate to those who fear him.
> For he knows how weak we are;
>   he remembers we are only dust.
> Our days on earth are like grass;
>   like wildflowers, we bloom and die.
> The wind blows, and we are gone—
>   as though we had never been here.
> But the love of the LORD remains forever
>   with those who fear him.
>
> PSALM 103:13-17, NLT

We hold on to the truth that God's love is eternal, and through that love He has given us eternal life. But there's no sugarcoating the fact that our life on earth is brief.

So what then? If life is short and loss is imminent, what is our response? As we walked away from Netka that day, the first thought that ran through my mind was *What about my brother? I need to text him and tell him I love him.* I can't imagine what Netka was feeling, but I know that if anything happened to my brother, I would be devastated. Yet I know that life is short and death comes to all of us. So what will we do with the time we have left?

What will *you* do? Will you grab your phone and text or call your brother? Will you forgive your dad, sister, or husband for past hurts that are coming between you? Will you say "I love you" to the people in your life who need to hear it? Will you do what you know you need to do in order to make things right?

What will you do? Whatever it is, I pray that today is the day you step out in faith and live—not merely survive but truly live—because tomorrow is not promised to any of us.

> Peace in the midst of loss comes when we see life for what it is, not what we wish it were, and by faith we enjoy, appreciate, and **celebrate the moments God gives us** because life is short.

7

One of the hardest things to do in life is letting go of what you thought was real.

UNKNOWN

As a result of Hunter's life and the creation of the Hunter's Hope Foundation, our family has had the incredible privilege of meeting families from all over the world. Heartbreak and loss have brought us together, but unconditional love and hope fuel the fire of our unique fellowship. We are one big, broken yet beautiful family.

Because of the nature of what God has called us to do through the foundation, we deal with loss on a daily basis. On some days we are on the receiving end of a frantic phone call from a parent who has just received the life-shattering news that his or her child has been diagnosed with a terminal disease and given only months to live. On other days, our amazing staff members are deep in the trenches of heartache, fielding end-of-life questions while helping families prepare for the inevitable.

With so many profound stories of finding peace in the

midst of loss to choose from, I had a hard time deciding what to include in this devotional. My friend and soul sister Christina from California—wife to Drake and momma to Judson and Jessie—was on my go-to list. This woman's life résumé is impressive. She is the CEO of Judson's Legacy—A Ministry of Faith and Hope in Suffering—plus she's a women's pastor and a prolific author and speaker. In addition to these accolades, Christina is a blast to be around. Her joy is contagious, and she is one of the most genuine and compassionate people I know.

After some prayer and gentle prodding, Christina agreed to share her heartbreak and hope with us.

It was a sunny summer day, but the gloom in our hearts was hanging thick in the air as we sat around a conference table, surrounded by doctors, waiting to hear the definitive diagnosis for our son, Judson, as he played with his bright green truck on the laminate tabletop. . . . The words of the doctors struck us with life-altering force. Terminal! Judson had a terminal genetic disease. He was never going to get better; he was only going to get worse. Just four months later my precious boy, not quite three years old, passed away.

It didn't take long after my son died for disillusionment to settle into my heart. I had ascribed, for much of my life, to the goodness of God, His love, and His perfect plan. But my experience of watching my beloved son suffer, holding him as he breathed his last, and living in his absence, suddenly called into question all I had once believed; my idealistic, underdeveloped understanding of the gospel was suddenly challenged by the sober realities of living in a fallen, broken world full of suffering and pain.

Disillusionment is the tension that arises when we must unexpectedly face the illusions that have been shaping us. And that's what they are—illusions—false assumptions—lies. These are things that we have believed to be true but are, in fact, misconceptions about life. Disillusionment is painful. It dramatically cripples erroneous notions that have unwittingly strolled into our worldview. But the value to be found in disillusionment is that we squarely face our misunderstandings about God and this world, giving us opportunity to discard our incorrect ideas and make way for a more full and robust picture of the truth. We have the chance to shed the mirage of illusion and anchor ourselves more securely in the solid reality of God's character and His Kingdom. Yet this takes courage.

We have a choice when we are disillusioned in the face of loss. Do we allow our hearts to be shaped and molded by a God who cares deeply for us but whose ways confound us, or do we cling even more tightly to our illusions? If we are unwilling to allow the pain of our loss to dissolve the lies in our hearts, it can lead to cynicism; we can become embittered that the world isn't the way we've understood it to be—that God doesn't fit the box we created for Him. This is not the path to peace.

Peace comes through shedding the illusions. Our understanding is limited, finite, and fallible, and so we desperately need a peace that surpasses our imperfect understanding, a peace that invades those broken places, protects our hearts, and leads us closer to the truth. This requires us to throw out our God-shaped box and allow Him to roam freely in our hearts without constraint. It creates the space for Jesus to occupy our deep wells of pain, where we are anxious, confused, broken, and discouraged, and permeate our thoughts with His grace and truth, which ultimately leads to peace and joy.

Yet, such a transformation in brokenness must arise out of a humble posture that acknowledges the greatness of God and our inability to fully comprehend Him. In Isaiah 55:9, God's ways are described as far grander and more splendid than our own. We need to approach our disillusionment with an attitude that marvels at the incomprehensible nature of God and our inability to understand Him, while submitting to His sovereignty over all things.

My God-shaped box was obliterated in the loss of my son. I realized God's goodness, love, and perfect plan wouldn't necessarily feel good, loving, or perfect to me, and the values I had for myself varied significantly from the values God has for me. My ways were different than His ways. My thoughts were different than His thoughts. Through the loss of Judson, God began dissolving some of those illusions. Therein peace arose.

I don't know about you, but I had to reread and meditate on what Christina shared. Her insight is deep and convicting. My immediate response was *I don't want to live with any illusions—false perceptions about life, myself, or God.* And yet by nature I often try to protect my heart at all costs. However living with illusions is hurting me and costing me way more than I realize.

Loss calls into question everything we believe to be true. When we're not sure what is real, we can go to Scripture to remind ourselves of the ultimate truth. In the book of John, Jesus emphatically proclaimed,

I am the way and the truth and the life.

JOHN 14:6

He also said,

If you hold to my teaching, you are really my disciples. Then you will know the truth, and the truth will set you free.

JOHN 8:31-32

We cannot know the truth apart from Christ. We cannot walk in freedom if we do not know the truth.

Loss has a powerful way of reminding us that the perfect family, great job, nice house with a white picket fence, "American dream" kind of life is not reality. Neither is a God who gives us anything we want, whenever we want it, and shelters us from all the heartbreak and pain in this world. Yet in shattering our illusions, God seeks to draw us closer to Himself, the truth, and His love.

He loves us too much to let us see Him as something He is not, or see ourselves as something we are not. It's not that He wants suffering, heartbreak, and pain for those He loves, but He will use all of the above to bring about a confrontation with reality, truth, and good—even when, as Christina said, it doesn't necessarily feel good. The process is often painful, but true peace comes as a result.

Peace comes as we allow the incomprehensible love and nature of God to **dissolve all our illusions**.

8

Suffering always confronts us with the fact that our lives do not operate according to our plans.

PAUL DAVID TRIPP

My cousin Josh was really handsome; I can still see his rugged features and dazzling smile. I wish I remembered more about him, but my memories are somewhat hazy because we were so young. But I do remember that he loved God and he was one good-looking young man who turned heads without trying.

Josh was one of my mother's many nephews. She comes from a family of ten siblings—eight girls and two boys—so when all of us showed up for holidays, we just about needed a stadium parking lot to hold all the aunts, uncles, and cousins.

I was at the top of the pecking order, the oldest of twenty-three cousins. Josh fell somewhere in the middle and, like many of the others, sort of got absorbed in the sea of family faces. When he was in his late teenage years, however, he found that certain something that made him stand out—drugs, and lots of them. Josh struggled with drug addiction for the rest of his life. His mom, my aunt Mary (who just so happened to be one of Hunter's home care nurses), tried desperately to break the power of the addiction in Josh's life. She sought counsel and intervened in every way she possibly could to help her despairing son overcome his problem. Nothing worked.

On a bright, beautiful autumn afternoon, while everyone else went about their daily routines, Josh took a shotgun and walked out into some obscure woods near the town we all lived in. There, he turned the gun on himself and took his life.

He didn't leave a note explaining why he felt driven to do such a horrific thing. There were no telltale signs or obvious indicators that something was dreadfully wrong other than the uphill battle he had been fighting against addiction. In fact, days before he committed suicide, he was seen in the local park preaching the gospel message to anyone who would stop and listen.

What I remember most vividly about this tragedy was my aunt's anguish. You see, no one knew where Josh had gone, and he was considered missing for months. The police searched. We searched and offered a reward for information, but we found nothing. We continued to cling to the frayed strand of hope we still had—that maybe, miraculously, somehow, Josh might be found alive. But that's not what happened. In the spring, they found Josh's body.

There are losses and then there's suicide—and the two are very different, as are the types of grief they produce. I'll be honest: I'm having a hard time writing about this right now, and my heart hurts even after all these years. I've never talked or written about Josh, maybe because I've gone through my own brush with suicidal thoughts and it was horrific. I've learned through my own experience as well as Josh's death that the stigma of mental illness is alive and well. Most people don't understand that psychological illnesses are just as devastating, if not more so, than physical diseases.

* * *

People can live without a lot of things, but hope is not one of them. The world we live in is desperate for hope. We look for it everywhere, from our relationships and professions to our looks, style, intellect, and status. We see the movies, read the books, and watch the talk shows, all looking for scraps of hope. And when these don't deliver, we'll even turn to the darker side of life, buying into its promise. We sift through the bottom of the sewer trying to soothe our aching souls with drugs, sex, alcohol, violence, and more. And, like my cousin Josh, we will even look for hope in death!

Don't we need something greater than ourselves to be the answer? If we cannot find hope in humanity, then it follows that our search must take us outside ourselves. Thankfully, there is a God who is greater than we are, greater than our questions, our problems, and our darkness—a Savior who is able to save us from ourselves. A generous, loving Father who offers hope beyond everything this world has to offer. He reaches out to us from heaven in the person of Jesus Christ, and He graciously gives us new life, meaning, and purpose. The empty promises this world makes cannot compare to His promises.

If you are in the midst of the emotional and spiritual devastation found when someone you know and love takes his or her life, God *sees* you. It may sound trite, but it is not. He sees you and knows exactly what you need right now. He is your refuge, comfort, peace, strength, and hope. Psalm 56:8 tells us:

> You keep track of all my sorrows.
>   You have collected all my tears in your bottle.
>   You have recorded each one in your book. (NLT)

He collects your tears and records them. (Can you even imagine?) He sees and feels your pain.

If you have been blaming yourself, like my aunt did, you need to stop and surrender the blame to God. *It is not your fault!* Please stop heaping guilt upon your shoulders that God never meant for you to carry. Give Him the guilt, shame, confusion, questions, and all the other emotions you are experiencing. Please allow God into all that you are wrestling with right now. He is the only One who knows you and the depths of your pain.

I call to God,
 and the LORD saves me.
Evening, morning and noon
 I cry out in distress,
 and he hears my voice.

PSALM 55:16-17

Dealing with a loved one's suicide might be among the more helpless situations any of us will ever face. And in addition to the pain, you are acutely aware of what it feels like to be out of control. To know that no matter how much you have planned and prayed, you have limited influence over your loved one's disease, mental health, or choices, or sometimes even over your own circumstances. At some point, we all face the truth that there is so much of life outside our control—and yet we so desperately want to control it. But if we can surrender our desire to be in charge, we can find peace in the fact that God is in control, and He is much wiser than we are. What we cannot comprehend, He understands completely—and therein lies our peace and rest.

Peace in the face of loss comes when
we **surrender what we cannot control**
to the One who is in control.

9

*To live is to suffer, to survive is to find
meaning in the suffering.*

GORDON D. ALLPORT

OF ALL LOSSES, divorce may be responsible for more shed tears than even death itself. In many ways it is a type of death—so much so that its victims must grieve their way through it. While divorce rates have declined marginally in recent years, it is still among the most destructive forces to infest our culture. The truth is that no one is exempt from the many subtle dynamics that can erode a marriage. The issue of divorce is really the issue of marriage, what makes it strong and what undermines it. And no one is immune— even Jim and I came very close. I will share about that in a later devotion.

There's an old saying: "The bigger they are, the harder they fall." This is true with respect to divorce: The longer you're married, the greater the potential for heartbreak and loss. On the flip side, the greater the destruction, the greater the potential for healing, redemption, and the greater glory of God. Dave, a close friend of mine, suffered deep anguish after losing his marriage of more than twenty-five years, but eventually he saw God work great healing in the lives of his family members. Where once there had been destruction and loss, God brought unexpected beauty. Let me share his story with you.

From the very beginning, Dave and his wife were on fire for the Lord. They were involved in their church and missions and were passionate about sharing the gospel. They brought up their children in the Lord, showing them by example what it means to have eternal priorities. They didn't have a lot, but everything they had, including their lives, they gave with the hope that others might gain.

As time went on, though, circumstances and deep childhood wounds gradually caused their relationship to disintegrate. A medical condition inadvertently led to Dave's wife turning to devastating prescription drug abuse that brought alienation, hurt, and irreparable damage. Her addiction reached a point where the kids knew something was terribly wrong, and as a result, they, too, began to suffer. While Dave desperately tried to hold everything together, he watched powerlessly as the woman and marriage he cherished fell apart. Unfortunately, Dave's wife would not get the help she desperately needed at the time, and so he felt forced to pull the plug on a marriage that had been on life support.

In response to the divorce proceedings, she overdosed in

front of the kids and wound up in rehab. The darkness consumed her as she grew hostile, unfeeling, and heartbroken. After a couple of years of legal wrangling, the divorce became final and Dave walked away with the house, the kids, and a mountain of legal expenses.

Sadly, a family that was once on fire for God was now left in a heap of ashes. As always, the kids suffered the most, and Dave's main goal was to protect them. His own walk with the Lord suffered too, and it's fair to say that he went off road for a few years. Though it took some time, he has since come back stronger and more in love with Jesus than ever.

Dave and his former wife are now close friends, and more than once she has thanked him for what he did. Not only did his intervention force her to face some intense problems, it also led her down a path of wholeness and healing that might never have come to fruition had she not had to make it on her own.

Physicians have said that some bones, when fractured, heal even stronger than they were before the break. This reminds me of the cliché "What doesn't kill you makes you stronger." Dave and his wife experienced damage and even permanent scarring, but they emerged with a greater knowledge of God's love, forgiveness, and redemptive power than either of them had ever known. Dave watched in amazement as the Lord took the shattered pieces of his relationship and worked them all together for his family's good. He saw financial miracles, emotional and spiritual miracles, and more. He saw God align circumstances to benefit him, his children, and even his former wife time and time again.

And more than anything, he saw his unspeakable loss and heartbreak become a full and rich life. In many ways, I believe Dave became a living illustration of Isaiah 61:3, where the Lord promises to

> provide for those who grieve in Zion—
> to bestow on them a crown of beauty
> instead of ashes,
> the oil of joy
> instead of mourning,
> and a garment of praise
> instead of a spirit of despair.
> They will be called oaks of righteousness,
> a planting of the LORD
> for the display of his splendor.

When I read this verse in the past, in the midst of my own heartbreak and loss, I found it hard to believe that I would ever be happy or joyful again. I never imagined that grief could produce anything beautiful. But it did, and I believe with all my heart that God will do the same in your life. Of all the blessings birthed through grief, the greatest has been a deeper appreciation for the gift of life and the people that God has placed in my life to love for such a time as this.

Divorce is destructive on many levels, and the resulting

loss can cause deep pain for years. And yet our God, in His uncompromising, unconditional love, can take circumstances that tend to bring out the worst in us and, instead, bring out our best.

Have you suffered a traumatic loss, whether it's divorce or something else? Do you know someone who has? When God is involved, even the most devastating circumstances can be used for good. He can and will transform ashes into beauty, mourning into dancing, and despair into praise. He's God! Nothing is too hard for Him.

> Peace in the midst of loss comes when **we trust God to create something beautiful** out of our brokenness.

10

It's not the load that breaks you down,
it's the way you carry it.

ATTRIBUTED TO LOU HOLTZ

IT HAS BEEN SAID that if you can count your true friends on one hand, you are blessed. If that's the case, my husband and I are profoundly blessed to count Joe and April as true friends. Sadly, they are "well qualified" to explain how loss can dramatically change a life. I'm going to let them (Joe first and then April) do most of the talking because I think you'll find that what they have to say will matter to you just as much as it matters to me.

Our first son, Joey, was born with normal diagnostics, but soon everything changed. My wife called me panicking one day because little Joey had had a seizure. We went to the emergency room, and he was admitted to the ICU, where the doctor confronted us with these haunting words: "Your son has microcephaly and his brain did not grow. He will never be normal."

When a parent gets this type of news, their entire world falls apart. With disabled children, the loss is just beginning, and will intensify, becoming worse with time.

Our greatest fear was wondering, "Who will take care of Joey if something happens to us?" So April and I decided to have another child who would be there to care for Joey. We were told that Joey's situation was a genetic mutation and that it happening again would be like winning the lottery twice. Thus we decided to have another child, and my son Evan was born, again with normal diagnostics. Unfortunately, Evan developed the same syndrome as Joey and it all began again.

So how do I deal with loss? Among other things I look to my wife because she is a pillar of strength. Personally, I run the entire gamut from "Why me?" to "Why them?" I have experienced rage, depression, hopelessness, jealousy, and many other emotions. I must admit that a large part of me died when Joey and Evan were diagnosed. There is nothing I can do to change the course of their lives, so rather than focus on what I cannot do, I focus on what I can do for them. My boys are amazing and I love them, but it still hurts. And I imagine it always will.

I appreciate Joe's honesty. He shared his raw emotions when a lot of guys, my husband included, find it really difficult to go there. I commend him for that and hope it inspires you to do the same, regardless of the good, bad, and ugly you might be dealing with right now.

The solidarity I feel with April comes from the common heartbreak we share. I'll let April share her side of things with the hope that her words resonate in your heart like they have in mine . . .

Men and women handle loss differently, and though we both deeply love our boys, Joe and I have processed our losses in very distinct ways.

When Joey was about five years old, I asked a specialist about the life expectancy of our boys. He told me that the average life expectancy of a healthy person is eighty years. If you take a healthy person who becomes nonambulatory, you cut their life in half. If you take that same person and put a foreign object into their body like a feeding tube or tracheostomy, you cut their life expectancy in half again. And if that person is institutionalized, they probably won't live to be ten years old.

I was shocked, and since then I have lived every day to make sure Joey and Evan receive the best care possible.

This journey has taught me many things. First

and foremost, I truly believe with all my heart that we each have a choice to make when we wake up every morning. We can choose to be thankful and make every moment count, or we can feel sorry for ourselves and crawl back in bed. I choose to make every day the best I possibly can, and I feel like every moment I am given with my boys is a gift.

April's love and resolve inspire me. I know what it is like to care for a severely disabled, terminally ill child, but I can only imagine what it would be like to be the mom of two. I have witnessed her and Joe in action *living* the unconditional love they have for the boys, and it is beautiful and heartbreaking. Joe and April's love, determination, and perseverance exemplify 1 Corinthians 13:7:

[Love] always protects, always trusts, always hopes, always perseveres.

I appreciate April's conscious choice to be thankful and cherish life regardless of the heartbreak. Her desire to make the most of the time she has been given with her sons is admirable and convicting. Let's be real: Haven't we all faced this battle? Haven't we had times when choosing to get out of bed and go the extra mile felt too difficult, making the easy way out look so much better and more fulfilling? However, lest we forget—both choices come with a cost, one greater than the other.

Maybe you are tired of trying so hard and yet feel like you have no other choice. Please allow me to remind you that you *always* have a choice. The fact that you have chosen the road less traveled in order to fully live in each moment, regardless of the circumstances or personal cost, says a lot about your character. And although you might think that no one notices your efforts or sees your struggle—God sees you. He knows. Furthermore, He appreciates your willingness to pay the price. And regardless of how you feel, He is with you every step of the way.

If 1 Corinthians 13:7 describes Joe and April's attitude toward caring for their children, the first part of verse 4 characterizes the loving heart they have for them. It simply says, "Love is patient, love is kind." That is not what they do; it is who they are. That is who God is too, and it is who we can aspire to be. My understanding of this type of godly, unconditional love is that it always seeks the highest good of the object of its affection above all else. Love is a choice!

Whether you're in the midst of caregiving, like Joe and April, or you're dealing with another loss that seems to go on and on, you always have a choice. A choice to make the best of your circumstances. A choice to appreciate your life—or take it for granted. A choice to be selfless—or selfish. And when you boil all that down, one simple question remains: Like Joe and April, will you choose to love and make the most of every moment?

Peace in the midst of heartbreak and loss can be found in **choosing to make the most of every moment** regardless of your circumstances.

11

Praise the LORD. Give thanks to the LORD,
for he is good; his love endures forever.

PSALM 106:1

ALLOW ME TO INTRODUCE you to my nephew, Zac Kelly. Zac, the firstborn son to my husband's younger brother Danny, is presently nineteen years old and the eldest of four boys. Danny and his wife, Kathleen, had their four sons but decided they weren't going to stop trying until they got their girl, which they did—Faith, the only daughter. No wonder they named her Faith. I imagine after having four sons, Dan and Kathleen just might have prayed a little bit harder and longer for a daughter. If you have a house full of boys, you know what I'm talking about—lots of smelly socks and loads of testosterone.

Eleven days before our son, Hunter, was born, baby Zac came into the world. I'll never forget when Jim and I went to the hospital to visit the newest rookie on the Kelly roster.

I was nine months pregnant with Hunter, and my belly was bursting at the seams. At the time, I was also the only one who knew that we were having a boy. Jim had no clue, and I wasn't about to ruin the surprise. When I held little Zac in my arms and looked into his beautiful eyes, I couldn't help but think about the baby boy growing in my womb. I wondered what he would look and feel like as I touched Zac's soft skin and held his tiny hands. In a way, the joy of cuddling Zac was even greater because I knew that soon I would be holding my own son.

As you can imagine, after Hunter was born, Jim and Danny went back and forth talking about all the great things they had planned for their sons. Jim believed that Hunter, like his daddy, would become the stellar quarterback throwing perfect thirty-yard spirals to his wide receiver cousin Zac. As God would have it, Zac is presently a wide receiver for his college football team, and he's really good. Kelly boys are just that, Kelly boys—and with that last name come some serious expectations of athleticism, character, and toughness.

As the baby boys continued to grow, Jim and Danny would discuss the milestones their sons were achieving. Or in Hunter's case, the milestones he was unable to achieve. Zac was starting to hold his head up on his own, play with toys, and babble a bit while Hunter cried often and had difficulty eating. Eventually, the unachieved milestones, eating issues, and irritability led to a slew of doctors' visits and tests. On June 24, 1997, our worst nightmare came true when our son was diagnosed with a fatal genetic disease. Danny was there the day Hunter was born and he was there the day he was diagnosed. In an instant, all the shared hopes and dreams that Jim and Danny had for their boys vanished.

I vividly remember the days when Kathleen would bring Zac over to our house for visits. Zac was smiling and active. Hunter never smiled and could not move on his own. Zac was full of life. Hunter was dying. Every time I was around Zac my heart hurt. I'm crying as I write this just thinking about it. I wasn't walking by faith or trusting God with my pain during those days, so jealousy and resentment took root in my heart. Honestly, I desperately wanted what Kathleen had—a healthy son. That might seem horrible, but it's true. It took the love and grace of God for me to realize that my son was a blessing, not a burden; that his life was a treasure, not a tragedy. For a time and until God intervened in my life, I'm sad to say I could not be around Zac. Staying away from him meant protecting my heart, and at the time, as awful as it sounds, the instinct for self-preservation trumped everything else.

While Hunter continued to suffer day after day, Zac was growing up, doing all the fun things boys do. For the eight and a half years that Hunter was alive, I watched Zac's life unfold from a distance. The boys would get together on birthdays and holidays, but that was about it. In retrospect I wish my heart had been in a better place during those days, because Hunter would have loved spending time with Zac. As Zac got older, he eventually developed a love for hunting and a passion for football like his uncle Jim. When he was old enough, Uncle Jim got him his first camouflage outfit and 20-gauge shotgun and signed him up for his hunter safety course. And of course Uncle Jim was there when Zac shot his first turkey and buck. Today, they have an amazing relationship, much like what I envisioned Jim would have with Hunter.

I have been writing this particular devotion during the twenty-ninth annual Jim Kelly Football Camp. Yesterday was the final day of camp as well as closing ceremonies, so I decided to stop in and check out all the action. While I was there, my nephew Chad was throwing the football to Zac. While watching the boys do their thing, I couldn't help but think about Hunter and what it would be like if he were there with the rest of the Kelly boys.

In moments like this, I could watch Zac and the rest of my nephews and walk away filled with sorrow, resentment, and jealousy. How horrible and depressing. Don't get me wrong; I still get sad sometimes when I'm around all the Kelly boys. My heart still hurts, especially for Jim. But I don't stay in the valley of sorrow. Instead, and by God's grace, I choose to see my loss through a heart of gratitude. I am so thankful for the multiple ways in which God has used Zac's life to bless our family and breathe renewed hope and joy into Jim's life.

No, I will never know what it's like to watch my son toss the football around with his cousins. (However, I do believe that once we are all in heaven together anything is possible, even football with Jesus.) But what I do know is that God blessed our family with eight and a half amazing years with our son. Every moment of every day was a gift. He also blessed us with Zac Kelly. And every moment with him is also a gift from God.

The truth is, I have a choice—and you do too. We can choose to be thankful for the many blessings we have been given in the midst of our heartbreak, or we can choose to be ungrateful and miserable. It's really that simple. As the apostle Paul wrote to the Thessalonians,

> Rejoice always, pray continually, give thanks in
> all circumstances; for this is God's will for you in
> Christ Jesus.
> 1 THESSALONIANS 5:16-18

This is God's will for us because it is best for us. Gratitude leads to more gratitude. When we choose to live with thanksgiving, our lives will contain more joy and more contentment. And more peace. Even our heartbreak will be eased because we will understand more fully that God is with us.

What are the blessings in your life? What can you thank God for right now?

> Peace comes when we choose to
> **be thankful in all circumstances.**

12

Never be ashamed of a scar. It simply means you
were stronger than whatever tried to hurt you.

UNKNOWN

A GOOD FRIEND of mine has a cousin who has been through a tremendous battle with both lung cancer and breast cancer. She lost an awful lot but found a way to walk in peace through one of the darkest valleys. Her courage under fire, indomitable spirit, and abiding resilience—coupled with humility and vulnerability—are truly the stuff of heroes. I think you'll appreciate her story.

Dawn has been employed by a major financial institution for decades, working her way up to executive assistant for one of the company's vice presidents. She is smart and energetic, is very successful in the workplace, and is a devoted mother to two grown children. A few years ago, Dawn developed a cough that wouldn't quit. After the usual course of antibiotics and other medications, her physician ordered a biopsy just to be safe.

The results weren't so safe, and when Dawn got "the call," her doctor told her to get into an oncologist's office first thing in the morning—she had lung cancer. Thankfully, one of Dawn's friends, a practicing oncologist, got her in to be examined immediately and set up the appropriate regimen of chemo. A cousin had recently died of kidney cancer, which made her own diagnosis and subsequent treatments even scarier and more intimidating. As you can imagine, she didn't know what to expect. Would she get sick? Lose her hair? Lose the ability to work? Would she die from cancer—was the clock ticking?

There were so many unknowns to wrestle with and so much to lose in the struggle, yet Dawn's sense of frailty and hopelessness gave way to an ironclad resolve to do everything necessary to beat the onslaught. She grappled with sorrow, stress, anxiety, fear, and intense fatigue, and her toughest moment was telling her family that she had cancer. And yet, her positive attitude and unyielding confidence were contagious, overflowing into the lives of everyone around her.

Then, in the thick of everything, the doctors discovered that she also had breast cancer, and she ended up having a double mastectomy. As you can imagine, after a double mastectomy, chemotherapy, and radiation, Dawn was completely drained. In addition to riding a roller coaster of emotions, on a daily basis she would stand before the mirror looking at herself: scarred from the full mastectomy, totally bald, weak, and weary. Yet, regardless of what cancer was trying to throw at her, Dawn was filled with deep, abiding joy and gratitude. She was and still is quick to say without reservation that God was by her side, strengthening her and carrying her during the most difficult time of her life.

Today, Dawn has a head full of hair and a heart full of thanksgiving. Although she continues to manage a considerable amount of pain, she's back at work and living life—not merely surviving cancer. She has come to value every moment of every single day as a gift from God, and while Dawn still plans for tomorrow, she no longer takes today for granted.

Dawn's battle has caused her to do a lot of reflecting. "It doesn't bother me anymore when I see all my scars," she shares with a joyful sigh. "It's my journey, and I have no regrets." She continues, "I think each and every experience has been a difficult one, but you have to fight and you have to do it well."

I came across a great quote by an unknown author that I think sums up Dawn's message. And hopefully it will encourage, inspire, and motivate you:

After a while I looked in the mirror and realized
. . . wow, after all those hurts, scars, and bruises,
after all of those trials, I really made it through.
I did it. I survived that which was supposed to kill
me. So I straightened my crown . . . and walked
away like a boss.

Dawn's fight could be yours, or it could belong to a friend, a family member, or even a friend of a friend who has been diagnosed with cancer. In my circle of loved ones, it was my husband and my close friend Mary.

While writing about Dawn's journey, I remembered having a poignant discussion with Mary while she was going through chemotherapy for breast cancer. She shared with me how she believed that God had chosen her to endure what she went through. "God handpicked me for this, and although I don't understand why, I am so thankful that He will use this cancer journey to allow me to encourage others," she proclaimed with conviction and joy.

What Mary said reminds me of a passage in James:

> Consider it pure joy, my brothers and sisters,
> whenever you face trials of many kinds, because
> you know that the testing of your faith produces
> perseverance.
>
> JAMES 1:2-3

Like Dawn, since she went through cancer, Mary's perspective on life's purpose and her priorities are now more focused than ever before. She is choosing to live by faith one day at a time, appreciating every day as if it might be her last.

Of all that I have learned from Dawn, there's one profound and thought-provoking conviction I continue to contemplate: "It doesn't bother me anymore when I see my scars." We all suffer loss, and we all have scars. Dawn's are visible, but most of us have scars that are just as real yet only seen by God. Dawn looked at her scars day after day, considering their meaning and their message. Sometimes we do the same. Over and over again we recount the wounds that brought the scars—the loss that birthed our heartbreak and pain.

But instead of just reliving the pain, we can learn to look to God and how He was faithful to us through that pain. We can think about how He has worked in our lives, how He has comforted us, or how He is capable of healing us fully someday. We can realize that we are different now, even stronger than we used to be before we had these scars. The scars don't have to be something we are ashamed of or regret; instead, they can point us and others to God.

Peace in the face of loss can be found when we allow our scars, both seen and unseen, to strengthen us to **live with no regrets**.

13

Sometimes you will never know the value of a moment until it becomes a memory.

ATTRIBUTED TO DR. SEUSS

FACT OR FICTION: *The older you get, the more you forget?*

Jim and I are both living testimonies of this fact. I usually forget little things like taking out the trash on Sunday nights while Jim's out of town, feeding the dogs, or turning off the outside lights before bed.

Jim, on the other hand, forgets more important things—like putting the seat down after he goes to the bathroom in the middle of the night so that I don't fall into the toilet. You laugh, but I have fallen in a few times, and it is *not* fun! Sometimes he will completely forget a movie that we have just seen or a conversation we recently had. Of course he has more legitimate excuses for forgetting than I do, like the numerous concussions he suffered as a quarterback in the NFL. His memory has also been greatly impacted by residual damage from the chemotherapy and radiation treatments he had to endure while fighting oral cancer. Consequently, he gets a pass when I don't.

Our ability to remember is curious and beautiful, but it's often a difficult gift, isn't it? A gift I have learned to unwrap with sensitivity and grace. It seems as though we remember what we would rather forget and forget what we wish we could remember. Do you agree? More often than not, we remember most vividly our pain and the circumstances or people that caused it, the traumas and trials we've endured, the battles we've fought, and the tears we have shed.

The memories of our deepest losses can remain raw years after the initial hurt. In fact, some of life's most shattering moments are etched upon our hearts so deeply that we can recount not only what happened to us, but exactly how we felt in those particular moments as if they happened just yesterday. Just as a swift, sudden physical wound like a burn or a gash takes only a moment to occur but a long time to mend, an emotional wound can befall us in an instant yet require years to heal.

I remember so many details about Hunter's life. And while most of these memories are amazing and good, what I remember most vividly are the painful experiences of my deepest heartbreak and most devastating loss. At the time of this writing, Hunter has been gone for almost eleven years. To be exact, he has been in heaven for 3,985 days. It's hard to believe that time rushes by so fast and we have been apart that long. Sometimes it feels like just yesterday, and sometimes my grief feels worn and weathered, like I have been missing him for hundreds of years. Not a day goes by that I do not think about him and miss him. The void he left eclipses words and resonates through my soul more than I could ever explain. If you have experienced the loss of a child, you know exactly what I'm talking about. Certain things just defy description.

I've come to realize that the good and beautiful that I remember about Hunter's life is mainly how I felt in the midst of those moments before they became memories. In other words, I don't remember specific details about shared experiences so much as I do the unconditional love and overwhelming joy I felt in the midst of them. Despite the suffering Hunter endured day after day, that mighty little warrior spread more love, hope, and joy than anyone I have ever met—simply through his presence and the unmistakable way in which God used his life to reveal His love. And the result was God filling our lives with more of His love and joy than we could contain.

Unfortunately, the memories that hurt the most I remember with daunting clarity. Like the day Hunter was diagnosed with Krabbe disease. The beautiful, warm summer day and bright blue sky as Jim and I drove to the neurologist's office. The sick, sinking feeling in my stomach and pain in my chest upon hearing what the doctor said and didn't say. The warmth of the tears falling from my burning eyes and running down my cheeks. The vacant, stunned look on Jim's face when we were told that Hunter would probably not live to see his second birthday. And the cold, silent ride home after we left the doctor's office. I remember it all and when I do, it still hurts.

It hurts because I'm still here. God hasn't called me home yet, and if you're reading this right now, you're still here too. You're alive. You have breath in your lungs and the rest of your God-given life to live. And you also have an abundance of memories of the ones you love and the losses you've suffered. Memories that heal and hurt. Memories you treasure and wish you could recall in greater detail, and those you wish you could forget completely. But both types of memories are gifts from God.

Before writing this I never thought of my memories as a gift. Yes, I have thanked God for all the physical reminders that prompt a memory, like our photos of Hunter, my journals that chronicle his amazing life, his Noah's ark books, and the many crafts he made while he was here. And yet, I have never before thanked God for my actual memories. As I do so now, as odd as it might seem, I'm just as thankful for the memories that hurt as I am for those that fill me with joy. They both tether me to reality in different ways, reminding me that life is short. They strengthen my perspective and help me to hope and stay faithful to what I know is true: the encouraging reality that this is not the end of the story.

It's not the end of your story either. God has more of your destiny to unfold. He has more in store for the rest of your days here on this planet and even more after you take your last breath. So much more that the Bible describes it like this:

> No eye has seen,
>   no ear has heard,
> no mind has conceived
>   what God has prepared for those who love him.
> 1 CORINTHIANS 2:9

What lies ahead holds more than we are able to imagine or comprehend. God has prepared an eternity of endless blessing for those who love Him. An eternity that includes Hunter and all the dear ones you love and miss so much. A forever life filled with God's presence and unending love. Just talking about it makes me heaven-hungry. It also motivates me to truly *live* the life I have been given.

So while we wait for the day when our life on earth is but a memory, let's appreciate the gift of the memories we have right now—the life we've already lived and the memories yet to be made.

Peace comes as we embrace and
give thanks for the gift of memories—
both the good and the bad.

14

*"For my thoughts are not your thoughts, neither
are your ways my ways," declares the LORD.
"As the heavens are higher than the earth,
so are my ways higher than your ways and my
thoughts than your thoughts."*

ISAIAH 55:8-9

GOD'S WAYS ARE HIGHER than our ways and His thoughts are higher than our thoughts. We believe this to be true because He's God, but sometimes things happen that leave us with lingering doubts. The pain and grief we experience can often cause us to question God's love. Life happens and loss hits home, and it all seems inconsistent with who we think He is. Sometimes, as audacious as it seems, we even think we would do things much differently if we had His power.

Our world is full of suffering, war, disease, famine, and death—and we'd put a stop to it if we could. Right? If we had the power to do so, we would end all the heartbreak. What we have experienced in this life leads us to question: If God is loving *and* He's all-powerful, then why do terrible things happen? We're not half as loving as God and certainly not as powerful, and yet we'd never let these heart-breaks continue—would we?

There's a life essential that I like to call my "reality check," and that's remembering that God is God. Period. End of discussion. And so we're left to make sense of the senseless, to try to respond instead of react, and to live by the truth that God is God even though He allows life to unfold in ways that seem contrary to His love. He is good, even though He has allowed evil to exist for the time being.

I wrestled with these questions on a daily basis while caring for Hunter, and I revisit them when I reach out to the many families dealing with the same devastating disease he had. My friend Rick grappled with these questions in a different way when he lost a friend on the mission field, and his story is worth sharing.

Twenty-one-year-old Kenneth (pronounced "Kennet") came to a mission base located on a thirteen-acre patch of cleared land in Belize, Central America. He was from Jamaica and one of the friendliest, humblest, and most forthright young men you'd ever want to meet. Ken could not read or write, so leaving his home and serving as a missionary in a foreign country presented its share of challenges. But despite these setbacks, he had a willing heart, a huge smile, and a great sense of humor, and he was eager to learn and serve. Rick said he had never witnessed anyone enjoy life and laugh as hard as Ken.

A few months after Kenneth arrived, the mission team he was on had some downtime while preparing to leave for an outreach to Jamaica. They decided to take a swim in the nearby Belize River. A few minutes had passed when suddenly everyone realized that Ken was missing! They all began frantically searching for him, and after a good fifteen or twenty minutes he was discovered about eight feet underwater, caught in a circular current.

He was pulled out of the river and rushed to the nearest hospital in Belmopan, the capital city. A visiting medical team from Canada, including an emergency medical specialist, tried desperately to save Ken's waning life, but they couldn't overcome the lack of functional medical equipment at the hospital. Eventually there was nothing more they could do except watch helplessly as Ken took his last breath on earth and his first breath in heaven.

After Kenneth's death, questions lingered in Rick's mind for years. Why didn't anyone see Ken go down? Why didn't he struggle and cry out? He loved God so deeply and had so much to give; why would God take him so young? The truth is, we'll never know the answers to these questions this side of eternity because, again, God's thoughts and ways are higher than ours. And the simple fact is that He holds the keys to life and death. He gives and He takes away. It's not our call—He is God.

Ken's story reminds me of another missionary, Jim Elliot. I had one of his quotes on my Twitter profile for a long time, and it's one of my all-time favorites: "He is no fool who gives what he cannot keep to gain what he cannot lose." Jim understood that his life was not his own; it belonged to God. Because he lived by this, he was able to give his life to the One who gave him life. In doing so, he gained a trust in God that he could not lose.

Not only did Jim Elliot grasp this reality, his colleagues and their wives did as well. And their understanding and faith were put to the test. The very people that Jim and his four comrades came to serve and evangelize, the Auca Indians, eventually murdered all of them. The insane thing about this tragedy is that Jim and his friends had guns. They could have defended themselves, but they were determined not to kill any Aucas. Why? Because they knew that none of the tribe members were ready to enter eternity, while they themselves were.

If you aren't familiar with Jim's story, you can read it in *Through Gates of Splendor*, written by his wife, Elisabeth. It doesn't end with death. In fact, Elisabeth, who served along with Jim, went and lived among the tribe for two years after his death and helped lead the very people who murdered her husband and friends to Christ. She not only made peace with God's decision, but she ran with it to His glory.

* * *

It's not easy, but we can find peace when God's decisions lead to our loss. We do it by focusing on who He is and remembering that He is good. Psalm 145:17 says,

> The LORD is righteous in all his ways
> and faithful in all he does.

And Romans 5:8 reminds us,

> God demonstrates his own love for us in this:
> While we were still sinners, Christ died for us.

When we cling to the truths of His goodness and love, we can let go of everything else.

My friend Rick eventually made peace with God's decision to take Ken. It wasn't easy, but it happened. And it can happen for you, too. No matter what you have been through and how you feel about it, you can make peace with God's decisions.

I'll leave you with a moving message from Elisabeth Elliot:

> If we hold tightly to anything given to us, unwilling
> to let it go when the time comes to let it go or
> unwilling to allow it to be used as the Giver means it
> to be used, we stunt the growth of the soul. . . . [What
> God gives us is] ours to thank Him for and ours to
> offer back to Him, ours to relinquish, ours to lose,
> ours to let go of—*if* we want to find our true selves,
> if we want real Life, if our hearts are set on glory.[1]

Peace in the face of loss comes as we **embrace the reality that God is God**.

15

Write like it matters, and it will.

LIBBA BRAY

THIS DEVOTIONAL YOU'RE HOLDING right now would probably not exist if it were not for my cousin Jessica. Jessica is my first cousin on my mother's side of the family. She and my brother, Jack, were born just five days apart, and they are two years younger than I am. Jessica's mother, my aunt Nancy, is one of my mother's seven sisters. Because my mother was born into a huge family, I have a lot of cousins, and I guess you could say that we made up a good majority of the population of the small town we grew up in.

Jessica has a servant's heart and is one of the godliest and most beautiful women I know. She's a loving and devoted wife and mother to five children (three girls and two boys), a hedgehog named Ollie, and lots of wiener dogs. Jericka, Jessica's oldest daughter, is the same age that my son,

Hunter, would be if he were still alive. Jessica and her husband, Richard, founded Ride to Recovery, a Christian ministry that uses mountain biking as a tool to share the love of Christ with underprivileged boys and girls and those struggling with addictions. I've witnessed Richard and Jessica in action, and it's amazing how God is using their lives and ministry.

After we found out the horrible news that Hunter was suffering from Krabbe disease, we realized we needed more help around the house. Jessica came to the rescue. As often as she could, Jessica would come over with Jericka and her oldest son, Jaden, and they all helped me with whatever needed to be done. Jericka and my daughter Erin (and eventually Camryn, too, when she was old enough) would do fun girl things all day while Jaden and Hunter played Rescue Heroes and read books about animals and creepy-crawly reptiles—all the stuff that little boys like to do.

Sometimes when Jessica came over, Jaden would bring his violin and the two boys would play music together. Hunter was physically unable to play instruments on his own, so we helped him play the piano, shake the bells, and tap the tambourine. And although he was unable to smile, the look on his face radiated a heart full of happiness; you could tell that he loved every minute of it. Eventually, the girls and everyone else in the house caught the vision and got involved, which led to us forming a Christian house band called the Hopesters. It was so much fun. What a blessing those moments were.

One particular day while Jessica was at the house helping me, Hunter was really struggling—more so than usual. At the time, he was on twenty-four-hour oxygen, and we had given him chest therapy and medication and intervened in every way possible to help him breathe better. Nothing helped. I was fearful that we might have to take him to the emergency room because we had exhausted every other option.

Usually, during intense, life-threatening situations like this one, I would slip into momma-lion mode and rise to the occasion. I never wanted Hunter to sense that I was the least bit worried. However, on this particular night, instead of holding it all together, I lost it. I fell down on the floor near where Hunter was lying and started weeping uncontrollably. "I can't do this anymore!" I cried out. "Why, why, why does he have to go through all this?" Just as I was about to cry out again, Jessica wrapped her arms around me, picked me up off the floor, and walked me around the corner away from Hunter.

"You need to go to your closet right now!" she demanded. I lifted up my head and wiped away the tears streaming down my cheeks. Just as I was about to respond, she boldly proclaimed, "Jill, you need to get in your prayer closet right now. If you can't pray, you need to write." She hugged me, squeezing me long and tight, and then walked back over to the bed where Hunter was lying. I did exactly what she told me to do. I grabbed a pen and a journal, and I went into my prayer closet. And as I started writing, I inadvertently turned the page into a radical new chapter of my life.

As crazy as it sounds, following Jessica's advice that day changed both the direction and the quality of my life. When she stepped up and presided over the emerging crisis with Hunter, she helped me realize that I needed to step back, get by myself, and pray. Journaling changed my life—and crazier still, I believe it can change your life too.

* * *

Let's talk about this for a minute. How many times have you desperately wanted to pray yet couldn't find the words or even the will? What about those moments when your tears do all the talking? We've all been there, haven't we? What if the next time you find yourself frantically searching for words and unable to pray, you write it all down? What if you grab the nearest pen and notebook and pour your heart out on paper?

Not only has journaling helped me unload pent-up feelings on a daily basis, it has also become a sacred time with God. I need to write and I need to pray, and when I combine the two through journaling it drastically changes my prayer life—and, by default, my overall well-being. Journaling has enhanced the quality of my relationship with the Lord, deepening my intimacy with Him. Believe it or not, it has also blessed my other relationships. Penning my prayers helps me organize my thoughts, better connect with my emotions, and chronicle both my requests and God's response to them.

Maybe you're thinking you don't have time to journal. I

used to think that too until I started journaling. Now I make time, no matter what, because it's worth it. Anything worth your time takes time, right? After journaling now for close to twenty years, I can tell you that every moment writing, every coffee-stained page, every emotion and thought poured out on paper has been worth it. The spiritual, emotional, and relational returns have far eclipsed the investment. My journals are now a wide-ruled treasure chest filled with year after year of the faithfulness of God. They are a keepsake of all that God did in the valleys of my greatest heartbreak and loss as well as in the heights of my greatest joys.

David, who used psalms almost as a journal, invites us to share everything with God:

> Trust in him at all times, you people;
>> pour out your hearts to him,
>> for God is our refuge.
>
> PSALM 62:8

So what do you think? Is it time for you to grab a pen and notebook?

Peace can be discovered in the valley
of loss when we take the time to
pour out our hearts on paper.

16

*I remain confident of this: I will see the goodness
of the LORD in the land of the living.
Wait for the LORD; be strong and take heart
and wait for the LORD.*

As I WRITE THIS, the imposing glare of fluorescent lights
is shimmering off the walls surrounding me. I'm sitting
anxiously in a waiting room in a New York City hospital that towers above the corner of East Seventy-Seventh
and Park Avenue. It's a hot, humid, overcast day in the Big
Apple, and the typical noisy hustle and bustle is alive and
well. I used to enjoy taking quick trips to the city, but not
anymore—at least not for the reason I'm here today.

Jim's most recent PET scans and MRI studies came back
inconclusive, so we immediately scheduled additional tests
and biopsy surgery to be certain that the cancer has not
returned. Since his second go-around with oral cancer, he has
been getting diagnostic scans routinely every three months.

He will continue getting them until he has at least a consistent five-year block of time with clear scans and no cancer.

A crew of doctors and nurses just piled in to take Jim to the operating room for his procedure. As we walked down the hall, Jim jokingly remarked to the anesthesiologist, "You better not be a Jets fan!" We all had a good laugh and talked some football, and then I kissed Jim good-bye as the hospital staff escorted him away. That kiss before surgery is always emotional, isn't it? Because the truth is, anything can happen and you just never know. I walked away from Jim and headed to the waiting room.

So here I am, waiting . . .

Waiting and praying . . .

Even though I know better, part of me wants to pretend like it's all good, no big deal, we've been down this road before and Jim will be just fine. Because the other part of me is just scared. Yes, I've been down this road before, but that alone tells me I have no idea what lies around the bend. Of course all the what-if scenarios cause me to be fearful. What if the results reveal that the cancer has come back? What if something horrible happens to Jim while he's under anesthesia? What if the doctors discover something new? So many unknowns, and so many things that can go so wrong while only one thing can go right—being cancer-free. So much to think about and pray about while I wait.

Waiting makes it worse, don't you think? It's as if fear feeds on the unknown. And the longer we have to wait, the more anxious and fearful we become as our minds race to try to contain what we do not know. Waiting gives our minds time to wander in different directions and get lost in the wilderness of all sorts of crazy thoughts and emotions that fill us with dread.

One of the most important things I have learned in the waiting I have had to do over the years is to use my waiting time wisely. I need to refocus my mind on what I know to be true. The unknown can be filled with ominous speculation, intimidating half-truths, and what-ifs that try to undermine our faith in God's character and sovereignty. We need to get rid of thoughts that lead to doubt and fear, and focus instead on the truth of who God is and how much He loves us. The Bible describes what I am referring to like this:

> We demolish arguments and every pretension that sets itself up against the knowledge of God, and we take captive every thought to make it obedient to Christ.
>
> 2 CORINTHIANS 10:5

With God's help, we can take control of our thoughts. We can focus on Christ and keep Him at the forefront of our minds so that all our other thoughts come through that lens.

My daughter Erin is kind of an old soul who has been blessed with wisdom and insight far beyond her years. In the midst of her father's battle with cancer, she wrote about her struggle with waiting. I think it sums up perfectly what I'm trying to say.

Although fear beleaguered my mind, deep down I believed with all my heart that my dad was healed. In the midst of the wondering and waiting, God granted me an indescribable peace. As I think back to this moment, I'm overwhelmed by God's grace. Overwhelmed by how He lovingly revealed to me the true longing of my heart—what I'm really waiting for: Him.

We weren't waiting on a diagnosis, a scan, or a simple phone call from a doctor to tell us the news that our hearts ached to hear—even though we were. Those earthly assurances are fickle and fleeting because someday people will forget the news headline saying, "Jim Kelly Is Cancer Free!" They will. It's the world we live in and that's okay. . . .

Our moments of waiting were rooted in our confidence in the One who was holding my father's very life in His hands. The One who has the power to heal and has taken the sting out of death.[2]

Just as I finish typing in Erin's last sentence, there's a knock on the door of the room I'm waiting in. Before I can stand, the doctor's assistant, Claudia, bursts in, joyfully proclaiming, "No cancer! There's no evidence of cancer. Praise God!" Without hesitation I jump out of my chair and respond, "Yes, praise God!" And so my waiting is over—or is it?

You can't go through trials such as the ones we have had to endure without both losing and finding the best and worst of yourself. And for the moment, I am waiting to discover what I have lost and what I have found through it all, trusting God with both.

🍃 🍃 🍃

What are you waiting for? Maybe it is direction for the next chapter of your life, or an answer to a desperate need that you have prayed about for months. Maybe you are in the throes of grief and you're waiting to feel alive again. Whatever you are waiting on, God knows the beginning and the end and every minute in between. People and circumstances are forever changing, while God is forever faithful. Thus, while you wait, God is lovingly laboring in the midst of every moment, doing His greatest work in and through you even when you don't realize it. He is the Alpha and Omega of everything, including your season of waiting. And when you focus on Him during your waiting, instead of whatever it is you're waiting for, you gain perspective and peace because you never wait in vain.

> I wait for the LORD, my whole being waits,
> and in his word I put my hope.
> I wait for the Lord
> more than watchmen wait for the morning,
> more than watchmen wait for the morning.

PSALM 130:5-6

It is good to wait quietly
for the salvation of the LORD.

LAMENTATIONS 3:26

Peace comes when we **trust that God is working** while we are waiting.

17

*God always prepares us for battles, even though
we may not recognize it at the time.*

JENNIFER MARCHESON

I HAD JUST SAT DOWN at my desk to write when my phone
vibrated with a text message from my dear friend Jen.
Before Jen became a close friend, she was a nanny for our
family. Jen did anything and everything for us with joy and
without hesitation. We trusted her implicitly and knew that
our children were safe with her. More important, however,
is the fact that Jen is a prayer warrior. She stood by me and
prayed with and for our family during some of our darkest
days. We have laughed and cried together, baring our hearts
to each other too many times to count.

Jen lives in North Carolina now, so unfortunately we
only get to see her once or twice a year —if that. Although
we miss her terribly, we are blessed with the type of relationship where we can go months without talking but when

we finally do, we pick up right where we left off as if no time had passed. She's like the little sister I never had, rock solid and the salt of the earth in every way. I thank God for bringing her into my life.

When I realized that the text I had received was from Jen, I dropped what I was doing and immediately read her message:

> Not sure why but felt I needed to share this with you. . . . A few weeks ago, God laid it on my heart to get CPR certified again. The very next morning, one of the families I nanny for posted the Heimlich maneuver on the fridge because her friend had just had to use it. I knew this was confirmation, so I reviewed the Heimlich maneuver a few times feeling there was a reason for it. A week later I was in Chick-fil-A with the other family I nanny for when one of the kids started choking. I jumped up, pulled him out of his chair and started performing the Heimlich on him. It took three times before the chicken came back up. Once I recovered from the shock of what had just happened, everything made sense. God had specifically prepared me for this battle. God always prepares us for battles, even though we may not recognize it at the time. I love how God has spoken and continues to speak to His children in such a timely manner and on such a personal

level! I know we've shared some of our most amazing God stories with each other and it still amazes me when I remember them. Not sure why I was supposed to share that but there you go.

I know why she shared this with me. It's for you. Yes, this is one of those amazing God stories that we love to hear and pass on, but it's also a reminder from God that you and I both need to hear.

God has already specifically prepared you for the battle you are in right now. He has purposefully orchestrated the events in your life leading up to this very moment. Do you believe this? You don't feel prepared, do you? In fact, you probably feel inadequate, ill equipped, and unqualified in every way. I understand completely. I did not feel prepared to hear a doctor tell me that my son would not live to see his second birthday, or to watch him breathe his last and slip into the arms of eternity. I did not feel equipped to hear that my husband had been given a 10 percent chance of surviving his second battle with oral cancer. In fact, I have never felt physically, emotionally, or spiritually equipped for any of the battles I have had to fight or the valleys I have had to walk through.

And maybe that's exactly what God intended. Maybe if I had felt prepared and confident, I would have trusted in my own strength and wisdom rather than in His. Maybe not being prepared allowed me to desperately seek after the One who is always prepared.

What if I told you that you don't have to *feel* prepared in order to *be* prepared? What if you considered the fact that it's not about how you feel but whom you trust? The apostle Paul expressed what I'm talking about in his second letter to the Corinthians when he passionately cried out,

> But [God] said to me, "My grace is sufficient for you, for my power is made perfect in weakness." Therefore I will boast all the more gladly about my weaknesses, so that Christ's power may rest on me. That is why, for Christ's sake, I delight in weaknesses, in insults, in hardships, in persecutions, in difficulties. For when I am weak, then I am strong.
>
> 2 CORINTHIANS 12:9-10

Paul's message goes against everything the world feeds us on a daily basis. The world tells us that we should boast in our strengths and hide our weaknesses, that we should try to get ahead through our own smarts or power or charisma and never admit that we need help. But Paul says the opposite.

This was a man who not only witnessed countless miracles but also suffered intense persecution, constantly putting his life on the line for the sake of spreading the gospel. And though Paul was courageous, strong, and brilliant, God did not invest in his strengths but in his weaknesses.

Paul persevered by intentionally walking in his weaknesses because he trusted in Christ, not in his scholarship, brilliance, or political connections. He was dead to his natural gifts—coming to his brothers and sisters in weakness, not wisdom; in the Spirit's power, not persuasion; and in fear and trembling, not in self-confidence (see 1 Corinthians 2:1-5). He wasn't enough on his own, but he pointed others to God, who was enough. That was how the Lord prepared Paul so he was battle ready for each moment. And that's exactly how He has prepared and is preparing you.

Do you believe that God has specifically prepared you for the battle you're in, just as He prepared Jen for the battle she faced? If you don't believe, are you willing to pray and ask Him to help you trust in Christ alone? I know it's hard. But you can decide today to rely on His strength rather than your own. To depend on His perfect knowledge and understanding rather than rack your brain trying to figure it all out. God knows your needs before you even become aware of them. He sees the depths of your pain and holds every fragment of your broken heart.

My daughter Erin's favorite verse is Exodus 14:14:

The Lord will fight for you; you need only be still.

If the battle belongs to the Lord, then your goal in this moment and every moment that leads you into eternity is to let Him do what only He can do. Because He is God and He is faithful.

Peace in the face of loss comes when we trust that **God has prepared us in advance** to walk into each moment because the battle belongs to Him.

18

*Finally, brothers and sisters, whatever is true,
whatever is noble, whatever is right, whatever is
pure, whatever is lovely, whatever is admirable—
if anything is excellent or praiseworthy—
think about such things.*

PHILIPPIANS 4:8

WHILE HUNTER WAS ALIVE, his continuous medical needs demanded an extraordinary amount of planning and preparation. We had to be vigilant about every detail of his life, including having a rigorous schedule that was meticulously documented and strictly observed every single day. In fact, I can go back through Hunter's schedule books and tell you exactly what he did and when on any given day. As you can imagine, these books are a treasure in retrospect because they chronicle my son's day-to-day life while he was still with us.

One of our primary concerns as we structured Hunter's life map was staying alert to everything he was exposed to on a daily basis. Because we were told that he was dying, we were determined to bring *life* into every moment God gave us with him. We did not want him just to survive each day; we wanted him to *live* in every good sense of the word!

We made every effort to protect Hunter (and his two sisters) from anything that would discourage or hurt them in any way. One way we did that was to keep the television and radio turned off, since the majority of what airs is negative or inappropriate. We made sure the children only listened to and watched encouraging music and movies, and we were also careful about our words. My mother, affectionately known as "Grammie," was so adamant about this, and so intensely protective of Hunter, that she created poster board signs and plastered them around our house like mini-billboards. The signs read: *Only uplifting and encouraging words allowed in this room.* She even brought the signs to the hospital whenever we were there and posted them outside Hunter's room. We were determined to protect Hunter from influences that were emotionally and spiritually harmful or discouraging. We put into practice Paul's advice in Philippians 4:8 to fill our minds with what is good.

While Hunter was still with us, he was a constant, visual, living reminder for our entire family and for everyone else who had the privilege of taking care of him. He reminded us to focus on the good even when nothing around us was going well. He inspired us to walk in an attitude of gratitude, striving to be thankful and content even when it was easier to be ungrateful and complain. He challenged us to care about the details of life as well as the choices we made. God taught us so much through Hunter, but one of the most vital life lessons we learned hit home as a result of his death.

After Hunter went to heaven, everything changed. Our living reminder to focus on the good was no longer there, so we eventually took the signs down and turned the television and radio back on. Unfortunately, we also slowly began to allow the very things we had protected Hunter from back into our lives. It didn't happen overnight, but it did happen, and as time drifted on, we began to realize that the battle for our hearts and minds was very real.

                   🍃 🍃 🍃

We can't shut out the world completely, nor are we supposed to. We live here, and the Lord has given us a command to "go into all the world" (Mark 16:15), not run from it or isolate ourselves! But as we go into all the world, it is our responsibility to determine what we will allow to shape our lives. Make no mistake; what we allow in will make us either more like Christ or more like this passing world. Romans 12:2 reminds us,

> Do not conform to the pattern of this world, but
> be transformed by the renewing of your mind.

We are either for or against Him, and what we choose to let influence us reflects whose team we're on. The value of guarding our hearts holds true for all of us on a day-to-day basis, but especially during a season of loss. There is only so much we can control, and among those things are the influences we allow to shape our hearts and minds. We have a choice. Loss is hard enough as it is, and allowing more hurtful and negative influences into our lives through what we hear and see only adds to the heartbreak.

Guarding my heart is being mindful and strategic, going back to what we used to do for Hunter. That means being intentional with things like listening to Christian music more than other genres, or renewing my mind through reading the Bible or an encouraging book instead of spending hours scrolling through my accounts on Instagram, Facebook, and Twitter. Yes, social media can be beneficial, but it can also be more harmful than you think. It can cause us to compare ourselves with others—whether that's their healthy families, easier financial circumstances, or seemingly loss-free lives. Comparison makes us feel our losses more strongly and can move us into a pattern of discontent. I can't remember where I saw this quote, but it's true: "Don't compare your real life to someone else's controlled online content."

Ultimately, I have had to choose to lose in order to gain—to walk away from worldly influences that reinforce temporal values that stand in stark contrast to God's eternal value system. It's always a choice.

Consider the wisdom and perspective offered in Proverbs 4:23, which advises,

> Above all else, guard your heart,
>   for everything you do flows from it.

In making every effort to guard Hunter's heart, ultimately I saw the wisdom in guarding my heart as well and took steps to do so—moment by moment. Let me encourage you to do the same. Start today! Ask God to help you be more vigilant about influences and more redemptive with your time. Fill your moments with all that is true and good. Go get some markers and poster board and create your own reminder signs. Make guarding your heart and mind a prevailing priority. When you do, I believe you'll discover that a well-guarded heart and mind filled with truth will bring the promised peace you desire and so desperately need.

Peace in the face of loss comes when we intentionally **choose to guard our hearts** by filling our minds with all that is true and good.

19

Trust takes years to build, seconds to break,
and forever to repair.

UNKNOWN

I WAS CONVINCED that Jim and I would divorce after Hunter died. Hunter had been the linchpin that kept our family together, and while he was alive, all that mattered to me was taking care of him and his two sisters. My relationship with Jim prior to us having children was rocky at best, but after we found out that Hunter was terminally ill, I didn't have time to concern myself with what Jim was doing. And what was worse, I didn't care.

Our priorities were surging in opposite directions. Mine, predictably, revolved around taking care of the kids, while Jim's priorities seemed to be everywhere but home—physically, emotionally, and intellectually. Even when he was home, he wasn't home. From the moment we were told that Hunter was going to die, Jim and I were headed down divergent paths as we dealt with our heartbreak and loss. Though we never talked about it, the chasm between us had grown far and wide. We were together for the kids—and then Hunter was gone. I thought for sure our marriage was gone too, so we both agreed to seek counseling.

It was during one of our counseling sessions, only a few short months after Hunter was gone, that a wave of heartbreak rushed in and almost swept me under for good. I remember the conversation as if it were yesterday . . .

"Wow, this is a lot harder than I thought it was going to be," Jim said haltingly, tears gathering in his eyes punctuated by a deep, drawn-out sigh. "Jill, I have not been faithful to you. For a long time, I have not been faithful. I would do okay for a little while and . . ."

He paused and took another deep breath. "I don't want to hurt you anymore." Another sigh.

I didn't know what to do. Shocked, I sat there in stunned disbelief, utterly incredulous at what I was hearing. As if losing Hunter was not painful enough. Now this . . .

As Jim continued to explain, I sat there and bawled. "Jill, I realize now that Jesus is the only one who can help me. I need Him. I don't want to lose you. I don't want to do this anymore. You don't deserve to be treated this way." Another deep breath and he continued. "Jill, I've asked Jesus to forgive me and help me." He turned his body toward me and looked directly into my tear-filled eyes as he said, "Will you forgive me?"[3]

Just thinking about that day brings back so much pain. And yet, without Jim's soul-deep confession and my resulting heartbreak, we would not be where we are today— together, in love, and better than ever. Don't get me wrong; forgiveness and healing did not happen overnight. It took a long time and a lot of prayer. However, God did intervene in every aspect of our marriage, and He is still holding us together. Let me say that again: *He* is holding us together. If Jim and I had tried to salvage what little was left of our marriage in our own strength and wisdom, we would not be together today.

Other than the devastating loss of Hunter, one of the most painful losses I have experienced was the loss of trust in my husband. Adultery, lying, and selfishness will do that. It will break down even the strongest relationships. When trust is absent, every other aspect of a relationship falls apart.

Check statistics and you'll see that most relationships do not survive infidelity. Add trauma or the loss of a child to the mix, and the statistics get much worse. Jim and I could have easily been a statistic. However, God has given us eternal hope and the daily grace and strength needed to persevere as a married couple one day at a time. He did and continues to do the impossible. And if you have lost trust in someone, whether it's a spouse, a friend, an employer, or a child, I believe He will do the same for you.

I have been asked on numerous occasions, "How did you ever trust Jim again?" The simple yet profound truth is that I did not trust Jim for a *very* long time. Instead, I chose to trust God with Jim.

You see, there is a dramatic difference between trusting God with a person's life and trusting a person. I began to learn this while Hunter was struggling to survive. There were so many serious health complications, so many doctors and opinions, medications, treatments, and therapies. It was scary and confusing, and I had a hard time trusting anyone to make all the right decisions—even myself. Eventually I gave it all, including Hunter, to God. I trusted Him to guide us one step and breath at a time.

I have done the same with Jim. Very early on I understood that I would not be able to emotionally, mentally, and physically carry the burden of not forgiving Jim. It was consuming me and eventually affected my overall health. With God's help, I was able to forgive Jim. I let go of my right to hold his sin against him, but I still wasn't able to trust him. That took much longer.

However, even though for a time I was unable to trust Jim—after all, he had failed before and it was possible he would fail again—I trusted God wholeheartedly. He has never failed me. I trust Him to do what only He can do in and through Jim's life. Just as I had learned to trust God with Hunter's life, I had to learn how to do the same with my husband.

Many verses carried me through the darkest days in my relationship with Jim. A few of them have been hidden deep in my heart, one of the most steadfast being Proverbs 3:5-6:

> Trust in the LORD with all your heart
> and lean not on your own understanding;
> in all your ways acknowledge him
> and he will make your paths straight.

I also found tremendous comfort in Proverbs 21:30:

> There is no wisdom, no insight, no plan
> that can succeed against the LORD.

You might not be able to trust the person or people who have hurt you. But you *can* trust God. You can trust Him to guard your heart and to bring the comfort and peace only He can in the midst of insurmountable pain and loss.

The loss of trust is devastating and at times debilitating. When you lose trust in someone you have given your heart to, the ramifications and brokenness are far reaching. However, God can reach farther still. He can resurrect, restore, heal, and make whole again. It is not an easy process, and it certainly takes time and prayer—but God is with you and for you, and through Him the impossible is possible. Jim and I are living proof.

Peace in the face of loss comes when you
trust God with the impossible.

20

*Because of the LORD's great love we are not
consumed, for his compassions never fail. They are
new every morning; great is your faithfulness.*

LAMENTATIONS 3:22-23

THE KITCHEN SOUNDED like a bustling barnyard as the kids
fell over each other to bring their breakfast dishes to the
sink, fill their backpacks with books and homework, and
double-check their uniforms. Lunch money was hurriedly
counted out and handed over, and they all prepared to pile
into the family van and drive to school.

Suddenly, my friend Jake felt his sweet, spunky six-year-
old daughter tug at his shirt. Her deep brown eyes pleaded
her case before a word left her mouth. "Daddy, I don't want
to buy my lunch today. Can you please make me lunch?" A
tired sigh escaped his lips. They were really pressed for time
and should have been out the door already, but how do you
argue with those manners coming from a kid that cute? Out
came the purple plastic lunch box to a chorus of laughter

and clapping from a pint-sized six-year-old. Sixty seconds, a peanut butter and jelly sandwich, and some improvised goodies later, he was her hero.

The three kids headed out the door, piled in the van, and buckled up. On went the engine and off went the family. He stopped the vehicle in front of the school's back door and watched as the kids slid the van door open, bellowed that they loved him, and piled out like a triple tornado.

Jake slipped his foot off the brake and was carefully drifting forward when he felt the van lurch over something huge. Suddenly, his son appeared at his side window, slapping it furiously. Jake rolled it down to be met by the horrific words "You ran over her!"

He slammed the van into park and tore around to the other side, where a crowd of children had already gathered around his daughter. She lay on the asphalt with a ghastly, distressed look carved into her face. He shot out orders immediately, sending his son to call an ambulance and his other daughter to push the crowd back. Looking at his little girl lying there, he took a deep breath and asked the one question that would make or break the rest of his life. "Honey, where does it hurt?"

He had no illusions. If she said "My tummy" or "My chest," he would have to bend down and kiss her good-bye. She would slip into shock any second, and no medical intervention could save her from the devastation caused by thousands of pounds of steel rolling over any part of her torso. She looked up at him and sputtered the most beautiful sentence he had ever heard: "It's . . . it's my leg!" Whatever the damage to her leg, he knew it wasn't life threatening.

On the way to the hospital, his older daughter explained what had happened. The kids had all jumped out of the van and she had slid the door closed, never realizing that the hood from her sister's jacket had gotten caught. As the little girl ran alongside the van and pounded on the door, her legs finally gave out and she slipped beneath the vehicle. Thankfully it wasn't moving fast, and only her one leg actually wound up in the path of the wheel.

At the hospital, the whole family waited to hear the extent of the damage done when the nearly two-ton van rolled over the six-year-old's knee. Feeling utterly isolated, Jake hung his head in his hands. In the midst of his own quiet struggle, he picked up his daughter's backpack, which he had grabbed in the parking lot, and noticed dirty tread marks across it.

He unzipped it and felt his jaw drop. There in his trembling hands rested a shattered purple plastic lunch box. The whole miracle suddenly came into focus, bringing with it a flood of peace that settled over his aching heart, soothing the pain away.

When he pieced together what might have happened, he realized that when his daughter's leg slipped beneath the van, the backpack—with the lunch he hadn't wanted to make—must have fallen between the moving wheel and her knee. The hard-shell lunch box had supported the enormous weight of the van just long enough for the wheel to rise up and barely glance off the side of his daughter's knee before the box shattered beneath the vehicle's weight. Had he refused to make his daughter the lunch she wanted, there would have been no hard-shell lunch box in the backpack, and the full weight of the van would have crushed her knee. The damage and related physical and emotional trauma could have been devastating.

As the full impact of the Lord's protection on behalf of his daughter and his family hit him, Jake heard himself proclaim out loud gratefully, "You're a covenant-keeping God, O Lord Jesus!" Though he was still holding his breath, he was not surprised at all when the MRI and other diagnostics came back clean. There was no discernible damage to his daughter's knee.

🌿 🌿 🌿

It is highly unlikely that you have or will run over one of your children—or anyone, for that matter. The world is full of tragedy, but thankfully that particular heartbreak is rare. However, we are all very likely to find ourselves cornered by circumstances that shroud our faith with doubt and fear. They can smother our belief in God and His faithfulness, and at times our doubt can cause us to live by sight rather than by faith.

This is when we need to remind ourselves of what the book of Hebrews says:

Now faith is being sure of what we hope for and certain of what we do not see.

HEBREWS 11:1

I like *The Message* version of this verse as well:

The fundamental fact of existence is that this trust in God, this faith, is the firm foundation under everything that makes life worth living. It's our handle on what we can't see.

We cannot see what's coming around the bend. But God can. Our circumstances do not govern the universe, preside over the destinies of nations, or determine the paths our lives will take. God does. There may not always be a lunch box that slips strategically between the unthinkable and a loved one, protecting him or her from disaster. But there will always be the love, compassion, and faithfulness of a God who will never forsake His promises to humankind. And that is where true and lasting peace is found—in knowing and trusting that despite our losses, God is still on His throne. He is still calling the stars out by name and numbering the hairs on our heads. Although we might not understand His ways, we can choose to trust His heart by faith.

Peace in the midst of loss comes when we **rest in the reality of a promise-keeping God** who faithfully cares for us in every circumstance.

21

Grief only exists where love lived first.

FRANCHESCA COX

I'M A MEMBER OF A SORORITY I never pledged or wanted to join, one made up of mothers who have survived the death of a child. I say *survived* because if you have buried a child and you are still breathing, still living, you are a survivor. Those of us in this group have been brought together by our greatest losses and deepest heartbreaks. We are a family. We speak the same language without using words—a language only we can understand fluently. We know when to speak and when to stay silent. We hug longer and cry often. The depth of our pain runs deep and draws us into a community built on a resilient foundation of trust, love, understanding, compassion, and loyalty.

My sorority "sister" Tammy Wilson is from Oregon, and she and her husband, David, have five beautiful children.

Tammy and David's third child, Marshall, was diagnosed with a fatal genetic disease when he was just thirteen months old. When Marshall was diagnosed, Tammy was in her last trimester, pregnant with her youngest son. Because Marshall's disease is genetic, meaning both parents carry the defective disease-causing gene, Tammy and David knew to test their newborn son as soon as possible. Their greatest fears were realized when the test results revealed that Michael had the same horrible disease as Marshall. Thankfully, because the disease was detected soon enough, baby Michael was able to get a lifesaving transplant. Today, Michael is a healthy, spunky little five-year-old boy.

I first met the Wilson family in the summer of 2011 at our annual Hunter's Hope Family and Medical Symposium for families dealing with Krabbe disease and other leuko-dystrophies. Every summer after that I had the privilege of snuggling with Marshall. In fact, my one-on-one time with him became a yearly tradition we both looked forward to with great anticipation. Until this year. Because Marshall won't be there—he is in heaven.

Four months after Marshall died and just a few days before the 2016 symposium, I received a text message from Tammy. We don't talk often, but when we do, we pick up right where we left off. Here's our conversation:

Tammy: I'm looking at Facebook memory lane and see pictures of you holding Marshall at symposiums in years past—so much love, so much heartache.

Me: Hi!!! Are you all coming this year [to the symposium]?

Tammy: Yes, all of us. [The whole family is Tammy, David, and their children: Melaney, Mason, Bryce, and Michael.]

Me: Ahhh, thank God! The girls have been talking about Michael! It will not be the same without Marshall. I can't wait to see you all.

Tammy: No, it will not be the same. Brokenhearted.

Me: That's how our hearts will look until heaven. Broken.

Tammy: I'll tell ya one thing, I don't understand this grieving process.

Me: Neither do I, and I suppose I just need to stop trying to figure it out. Or anything for that matter. It's too complicated and hard. I just have to choose to trust God. And try to live one day at a time. How are you?

Tammy: How am I? Trusting God.

Me: Sometimes it's just hard to keep breathing. But then the next breath comes. And the next.

Tammy: I agree. I'd love to look into the window of Heaven though. Just a peek. Just to see him. Just once. To see him healthy and whole.

Me: Ahhh, me too!!! And I have prayed for a glimpse of that in my dreams, but God wants me to wait until I see the real thing.

Tammy: I suppose it's the same for me.

Me: I'm looking forward to giving you a big hug
when I see you.

🌿 🌿 🌿

"So much love, so much heartache." This is life, isn't it?
No matter what kind of loss we're facing—loss of a friend
or family member, loss of an important relationship, loss
of a job—our lives are a mix of love and heartache. All
of us face it on this earth—including Jesus. In the Bible,
the prophet Isaiah tells us that Jesus was "despised and
rejected by mankind, a man of suffering, and familiar with
pain" (Isaiah 53:3). Oddly, I am comforted by knowing
that Jesus was familiar with pain and suffering because
that means He is able to understand and appreciate my
heartache.

John 3:16 is one of the most famous verses in the Bible—
often quoted and even written on massive poster board signs
at NFL games. It reads:

> For God so loved the world that he gave his one
> and only Son, that whoever believes in him shall
> not perish but have eternal life.

This was the staggering cost of God's love for humankind. Because of His love for you and for me and for all
people—past, present, and future—He gave us His Son.
And in spite of the widespread rejection He endured, Jesus
continued to love, heal, and forgive.

Jesus' life was filled with sorrow and heartache *because* He loved. And our love, which is an echo of His, will sometimes lead to heartbreak as well. Yet the authentic, true love we receive from God is a gift . . . a gift to be received and then shared. First John 4:19 tells us, "We love because he first loved us." And as a result of His uncompromising, infinite, perfect love for us, He willingly gave up His life so that we might experience true love—which here on earth is accompanied by inevitable loss.

Love and heartache. You simply cannot have one without the other. The loss of those you love can take many forms, with their passing being the deepest and most devastating. However, divorce, estrangement, rebellion, and a host of other lost-love experiences will bring about a depth of sorrow and grief as well. It all arouses the kind of heartache that you can feel deep in the marrow of your bones, the kind of heartache that silently echoes this inescapable reality: Where there is deep, overwhelming grief, there was great love. I would go as far as to say, in fact, that grief is the price of love—and it is well worth the cost.

Death leaves a heartache no one can heal. Love leaves a memory no one can steal.
FROM AN IRISH HEADSTONE

Each time we embrace a memory, we meet again with those we love . . . for the heart never forgets.
FLAVIA

Peace in the midst of heartache and loss
can be discovered when you
focus on the gift of love.

22

*The most incredible thing about miracles
is that they happen.*

G. K. CHESTERTON

I NEVER REALLY THOUGHT about miracles until I needed
one. Actually, now that I think about it, I have desperately
needed *two* miracles thus far in my life: one to save my
son and the other to save my husband. Both had received
death sentences. My son suffered from a rare, genetic, fatal
disease for which the doctors told us there was no treatment
or cure. My husband was diagnosed with oral cancer that
lurked dangerously close to his brain stem, giving him a
mere 10 percent chance of survival. Both needed healing
that lay well beyond human wisdom, medical resourceful-
ness, or anything this world has to offer. And both required
a miracle to get it.

God answered both of my miracle requests—one the
way I had hoped and prayed for and the other the exact

opposite way of what I had prayed for. However, both answers have been exactly what I needed.

Before Hunter was diagnosed with Krabbe disease, I never really thought about miracles or even God, for that matter. As far as I knew, I didn't need either one. I was raised in church, but faith and Jesus didn't mean much to me. I didn't practice or preach either in any way, shape, or form—they were irrelevant to my reality. When you're caught up in your own little universe, the things of God don't register much on life's radar screen. Thankfully, God knew me before I took my first breath or prayed my first prayer. And although I lived most of my early years apart from Him, He had His heart and affections set on me and my redemption.

After Hunter was diagnosed and we were told to take him home, keep him comfortable, and watch him die, you'd better believe I was all about getting that miracle. No matter what, no matter how, I needed a miracle for my son, and I was going to go wherever I had to go and do whatever I had to do to get one. Of course, it's not that simple, is it? You cannot text or call heaven and place your order—no, that's not how it works.

In hot pursuit of my miracle, I realized that I would have to learn more about the Miracle Maker. Through knowing Him more and reading His Word, I believed that somehow, some way I could obtain the miracle Hunter needed. Little did I know that in the midst of my desperate search for a miracle, I would come face-to-face with my greater need—Jesus. My prayer for a miracle was answered, just not the way

I had hoped it would be. Although Hunter was not healed on earth, he received full healing in heaven. In addition, our family was healed in ways we never realized we needed.

After Jim was diagnosed with oral cancer, I once again found myself facedown, on my knees, pleading with God for a miracle. And I'll be honest—because God didn't heal Hunter physically as I had hoped He would, my prayers for Jim's miracle were a bit jaded. I figured, if He didn't heal Hunter, why would He heal Jim? But even though I struggled with doubt and cynicism, my motives were sincere. God knew my heart and He knows yours. He sees the depths of who we are—the good, the bad, and the ugly—and thankfully He loves us anyway.

Even though I wrestled for a while with my jaded thoughts about miracles, I prayed daily for one. Despite the onslaught of lies bombarding my heart and mind, I continued to remind myself of what is true:

He performs wonders that cannot be fathomed,
   miracles that cannot be counted.
JOB 5:9

I spent time reading the Bible, focusing on the miracles that Jesus performed: feeding the hungry with a few fish and loaves, turning water into wine, walking on water, healing the sick, raising Lazarus and others from the dead. To counter my disillusioned understanding, I flooded my mind with truth.

My fervent prayers were answered, and God blessed Jim with healing. The doctor declared that it was "nothing short of a miracle," and he was right. God healed Jim, and it was a miracle. But what about Hunter? Well, what God did through Hunter's life was just as miraculous as his dad's physical healing. My daughter Erin pondered the two miracles as well as the prayers that were offered imploring God for them, and I believe she said it best:

> The greater miracle is found in seeking the Deliverer first and deliverance second; in longing for the Healer even more than the healing; pursuing the Miracle Worker before pursuing the miracle— the Giver before the gift. . . .
>
> With respect to my father, the greater miracle wasn't that the chemotherapy and radiation worked and that my father is now cancer free—although certainly this is a miracle, the one we prayed for. But the greater miracle is everything God did in the midst of it all to reveal Himself, draw us closer to His heart, and radiate His glory. . . .
>
> The greater miracle lies in recognizing that the setbacks in life are actually set-ups for God's grace and mercy to be displayed and magnified in the most unexpected people and places. . . .
>
> Ponder the greater miracle of finding joy in the midst of sorrow and suffering, or in recognizing that weakness is a bridge to the strength and power

of God that gives us the ability to be more than conquerors and overcomers. . . .

Or the miracle unleashed in truly realizing, like I mentioned above, that our need for the Healer is greater than our need for healing. . . . Or it can be found in the greater miracle that although none of us know what tomorrow holds, in this moment we can choose to trust the God who holds tomorrow and all that we don't know.[4]

Maybe, like me, you didn't get the miracle you were praying for. Maybe right now, as you read this, you are in a season of grief because loss came where you had hoped for healing. Whether or not you got the answer you asked for, God knows exactly what you need at all times.

Let's pray that He would help us to care more about who He is than what He will do for us . . . and to pray accordingly. Of course, we'll never stop praying for miracles, and sometimes we will receive them. But, as Erin said, let's pray that He would help us to long for the Healer more than the healing and the Giver more than the gifts.

> Peace in the midst of loss comes when we **love and trust God for who He is** rather than for what He can do for us.

23

There are three ways to learn from our mistakes:
the easy way, the hard way, and the tragic way.
The easy way is learning from other people's mistakes.
The hard way is learning from our own. And the
tragic way is not learning from either.

BRIAN HOUSTON

WE HAD JUST FINISHED singing a few worship songs and praying with our family and closest friends, and it was time to head into the church sanctuary to begin Hunter's funeral service. Although we were filled with anguish and deep sorrow, an overwhelming peace had filled the room and our hearts. It was as if you could literally feel God's presence, and as odd as it sounds, I did not want to leave. I wanted to stay where there was comfort and peace. Why did it have to end? Why did Hunter have to leave?

I didn't want to attend my son's funeral. I did not want to sit in the sanctuary a heart-shattered mess trying to comfort my two daughters. I dreaded the drive to the cemetery, and the thought of putting a casket filled with the beautiful body of my one and only son into the ground wrecked me.

I wanted so desperately to stay in that room with Hunter, to continue singing worship songs and praying. But I couldn't stay. I had to go.

When it came time to leave the preparation room to begin the procession alongside Hunter's casket into the church sanctuary where his funeral service (which we called "A Celebration of Life") would begin, a friend of Jim's approached us. We hugged in silence, and then he nonchalantly said, "Well, at least we can hope that he's in a better place."

The shocked look on my face in response to his attempt to comfort us spoke volumes, more than words ever could. Stunned, I walked away from the rest of the conversation in silence and over toward Hunter's casket. The overwhelming peace that I had felt just moments before began to fade, and I felt anxious and overcome with sorrow again. Like a broken record, his careless words played over and over again in my mind, reminding me of Job 38:2: "Who is this that darkens counsel by words without knowledge?" (NASB). To counter the lies, I had to remind myself of a Scripture-inspired saying I'd heard for years: "To be absent from the body is to be present with the Lord" (see 2 Corinthians 5:8, KJV).

I didn't have to hope that Hunter was in a better place. I knew he was.

Most memories of the funeral and everything that happened that day are sketchy at best. But there are certain things I can vividly recall, as if they happened yesterday. I remember that we all decided to wear white rather than black to represent life rather than death. I remember my youngest daughter, Camryn, who was just six years old at the time, clinging to my side and bawling during the entire funeral service to the point where my best friend, Karyn, had to take her out of the sanctuary and into the bathroom. I remember our nanny, Jill, with her incredible voice singing "His Eye Is on the Sparrow" and "Amazing Grace." I remember Jim taking deep breaths, trying desperately not to lose it in front of a church full of people. I remember watching tears stream down my ten-year-old daughter Erin's cheeks. And I remember the peace and comfort I felt as I stood near Hunter's casket and how the insensitive words from Jim's friend almost stripped it all away.

A lot of people said a lot of things during our family's darkest hours. Countless friends, family members, and even some acquaintances were comforting, encouraging, and compassionate when Hunter left us for heaven. Even so, ironically, the hurt lingers more than the comfort. Maybe that's because it takes a long time for deep wounds to heal and some wounding never seems to heal, regardless of the passage of time.

I'll bet every one of us has been on the receiving end of irresponsible and hurtful comments. We could swap stories of the wounds we've received from others' words. But we can do more than remember the wounds; we can learn some valuable life lessons from them. First of all, most people are clueless, including the person writing this. Our intentions are good, but our delivery and content need serious help most of the time. Haven't you said the wrong thing at the wrong time and walked away wishing you had never said anything to begin with? We're all guilty, and we all need grace. In fact, we need to practice what Paul said to the Ephesians:

> Let everything you say be good and helpful, so that your words will be an encouragement to those who hear them.
>
> EPHESIANS 4:29, NLT

I know it's hard to do, especially when we are hurting, but we all need to extend to others what we would hope to receive. When we're the ones struggling, we can ask God to help us forgive the careless comments. And when others are in crisis, we need to put ourselves in their shoes so that we can treat them the way we'd want to be treated if we were going through the same thing (see Luke 6:31).

Maybe you've been hurt by another's comments. Or maybe you've said some things that you had hoped would encourage a grieving friend or loved one, only to find that your words hurt instead. We need to practice patience with ourselves and with others. Remember, we are all learning, growing, and maturing into the image of Christ as we walk by faith each day. Furthermore, we all grow at our own pace based upon a varied roster of experiences, life lessons, heart-break, and joy.

> Gracious words are a honeycomb,
>   sweet to the soul and healing to the bones.
>
> PROVERBS 16:24

Peace in the face of loss comes when we **extend compassion toward those who hurt us** with their words, realizing that we could easily make the same error ourselves.

24

I have held many things in my hands,
and I have lost them all; but whatever I have
placed in God's hands, that I still possess.

MARTIN LUTHER

SOME CLICHÉS GET OLD. Although they may be full of wisdom, when you've heard them delivered hundreds of times
in various settings you might, like me, become jaded and
frustrated. Maybe you have stopped listening because you
are tired of people saying to you, "It will get better with
time." Or "He's in a better place." Or "You need to surrender all that to God and move on." And what about that
simple yet heartrending question "How are you?" My typical, cookie-cutter response has been, "We are good. One day
at a time. One prayer at a time. All in God's perfect timing."

As soon as I hear those words come out of my own mouth,
and as much as I believe them with all my heart, I sometimes
get annoyed with myself. Because the truth is, more often
than not, I am not okay; we are not okay. We are struggling.
We're sad. And sometimes I just want to be ugly-honest

and say what I really feel. But I don't. Why? Because we all struggle and we all suffer loss. Life is hard. And even though I believe that God is always good, *life*, on the other hand, is not always good. It is painful. It is gritty. It is unpredictable.

Okay, now that I have shared how I really feel, let's talk. Recently, I was in a group prayer time when one of those common clichés was discussed. (We call it a "prayer party" because that is what we used to call prayer time when Hunter was still here.) We had formed a circle of moms, dads, siblings, grandparents, friends, and sick children in wheelchairs with feeding pumps and suction machines in tow.

My friend Drake was leading on this particular day, so he started our session with prayer and then shared a few well-known verses from the Gospel of Mark:

> People were bringing little children to Jesus for him to place his hands on them, but the disciples rebuked them. When Jesus saw this, he was indignant. He said to them, "Let the little children come to me, and do not hinder them, for the kingdom of God belongs to such as these. Truly I tell you, anyone who will not receive the kingdom of God like a little child will never enter it." And he took the children in his arms, placed his hands on them and blessed them.
>
> MARK 10:13-16

Drake asked us to think about what we felt God was trying to convey through the writer Mark. One mom shared about being thankful that Jesus welcomed and loved children. She was glad that He rebuked the disciples for trying to keep the little ones away. Another mom talked about the beauty, simplicity, and vulnerability of childlike faith—and how children are so willing to trust because they have not experienced the hurts of this world that often cause adults to doubt God.

Drake's wife, Christina, is a women's ministry leader and mom to Judson (who has been in heaven since 2007) and his younger sister, Jessie, a thriving, compassionate, sweet nine-year-old. She began to share what she had gleaned from the verses, saying, "While my son Judson was dying, well-intentioned people talked to me about surrendering Jud to God. What does that mean? How are we supposed to surrender our children as well as our own lives to God when we don't understand what it truly means to do so?"

Maybe you have wondered that same thing. I know I have, so I was intrigued by what Christina was about to share. She went on to talk about how our children (specifically the terminally ill children and infants who were in the room) are a beautiful, living example of what it looks like in the Gospel of Mark for little children to come to Jesus and surrender to God. They are completely, 100 percent dependent upon us, their parents, for everything. They cannot talk, walk, or care for themselves on their own. They are fully reliant on us for survival. Our children trust us implicitly, without reservation or doubt. That is what surrender looks like. Surrender is realizing that you cannot survive without God. In fact, Jesus emphatically made this point:

> I am the vine; you are the branches. If you remain
> in me and I in you, you will bear much fruit; apart
> from me you can do nothing.
>
> JOHN 15:5

That's it! Surrender is vital to our relationship with God. Apart from Him, as He clearly stated, we can do nothing, including surrendering our broken, messy lives!

As the people at the prayer party continued to discuss what surrendering to God looked like to them, Drake chimed in. With a deep sigh, tears in his eyes, and a crack in his voice, he admitted, "I didn't surrender Judson or bring him to Jesus to get more of Jesus. I brought him to Jesus to get Judson back. But instead, Jesus gave me Himself and the tremendous blessing of the children and people in this room, which is more than I could have ever imagined."

Drake's heartfelt confession immediately brought one of my all-time favorite verses to mind:

> To him who is able to do immeasurably more than
> all we ask or imagine, according to his power that
> is at work within us, to him be glory in the church
> and in Christ Jesus throughout all generations, for
> ever and ever! Amen.
>
> EPHESIANS 3:20-21

It seems as though the greater blessing, favor, and peace of God in the midst of loss can only be fully experienced through surrender. As Christina shared, recognizing our complete dependence upon God is the pathway to surrender, and *that* leads to blessing. No, the pain of loss does not disappear when we surrender, but it can certainly be put into its proper perspective. In fact, our heartbreak, in light of the blessings brought about by surrendering to God, can actually be received as gain rather than loss because we know that God is able to do far more with our painful experiences than we could ever imagine. And isn't that one of the keys to the Kingdom in a sense? Jesus wanted us to grasp this when He said in Luke 9:24, "For whoever wants to save their life will lose it, but whoever loses their life for me will save it." Our loss is ultimately our greatest gain.

There is nothing easy about surrendering to God. Even after all these years and all that I have learned, I am still learning. Jim Elliot said it best: "One does not surrender a life in an instant. That which is lifelong can only be surrendered in a lifetime."[5] Perhaps you, like me, are something of a recovering control freak, surrendering daily. Each day—maybe multiple times a day—we need to stop trying to control everything and remember our utter dependence on God. However, I am convinced that the joy and peace we can receive in the process far outweigh the struggle of getting there.

Peace comes when we **surrender all that we are and have to God**.

25

*Now at last they were beginning Chapter One of the
Great Story which no one on earth has read:
which goes on forever: in which every chapter
is better than the one before.*

C. S. LEWIS

IT HAD BEEN A LONG and dreadful six weeks in an unfamil-
iar New York City hospital far from home. Our rigid daily
schedule included chemotherapy, pain medications, listening
to Jim vomit, radiation treatments, more medications, sleeping in the hospital chair, and a lot of crying and praying, all
compounded by various other family concerns. It was a season
that appeared to have no end in sight, and I prayed constantly
for the highly anticipated day when we could get Jim out of
the hospital and back home to Buffalo.

Home is where you go—it's where your heart longs to
be. For some of us who are deeply rooted in one place, our
home might be the most permanent possession and investment we have here on earth. Ideally, it's always waiting for
us with its safety, familiarity, and comfort as a shelter from

the storms of life. But even if the physical place doesn't stay the same, the sense of home can remain. And if there is one trait that most homes share, it is a welcoming environment where—regardless of the challenges or conflicts that might arise—hearts are knit together with love, acceptance, and forgiveness.

I found this to be true while Jim was going through his cancer battle, and it's also proven true when we gather with our Hunter's Hope family every year at the summer symposium. At our most recent event (the nineteenth annual Hunter's Hope Foundation Family and Medical Symposium), the room was overflowing with new and old families. There were fifty families in all, each representing a story of hope, loss, and heartbreak. Hugs were exchanged with tears of joy and sorrow against the melodic backdrop of noisy suction machines, feeding pumps, and sibling laughter.

My buddy Trevor had grown so much over the last year that I couldn't wait to hold him, touch his soft skin, and run my fingers through his thick hair. He was dressed from head to toe in his superhero best as Superman. He and his twin brother, Tyler, are seven years old now, and it's been two long years since their mom, my friend Nicole, died from cancer. Their dad, Steve, is amazing. He used to be a pilot but now takes care of Trevor full-time. My heart breaks for him because I know he desperately misses Nicole. We all do.

Some parents had lost their children a few weeks or months before, but in spite of their heartbreak they were still brave enough to attend the symposium. There was so much loss all around me, and yet, the love and joy we had for our children and each other overpowered the heartache. The pain was still there—we all felt it—but our faith and hope were greater still.

After our initial hellos and hugs, everyone settled down at their tables. We prayed together, ate, and fellowshipped, and then we did what we always do on the first night of the symposium—family introductions. We go in alphabetical order, so the Abner family from California went first. Their beautiful daughter, Katelynn, went to heaven in 2014. I remember her gorgeous long blonde hair, snow-white skin, and big blue eyes. She always wore colorful girlie outfits with matching nail polish, shoes, and hair accessories.

We continued the introductions, going from family to family. Eventually the microphone was handed to Kevin; he is Collin and Kendra's dad and Judy's husband. He's also a "Cheesehead" (a diehard Green Bay Packers football fan), a youth leader at his church, and someone who loves cracking jokes as often as possible. Kevin introduced his family and then said something I will never forget. "Being here with all of you is like being home. This is home."

His words played over and over again in my mind for the rest of the night, and as I pondered them, their meaning became vivid and powerful. Because of the love all the families have for one another and the depth of our mutual pain, all of us together make "home." It's the kind of home that is derived from common loss and a heartbreak that only people who have endured it can comprehend. It fosters a deep, abiding love and joy that we have discovered despite the distances and differences between us . . . a love that makes us feel like we are at home.

Any feeling of home, whether it's a physical place or a sense of community, is something else, too: a foreshadowing of our permanent home in heaven where every tear will be wiped away, love will forever abound, and relationships will flourish in a way we cannot even imagine as we pass through time. We will be reunited with our loved ones and walk in the presence of the Lord, in the midst of all the wonders He has prepared for us—none greater than being in His presence forever.

For believers, the "home" we experience here on earth is temporary. Aren't you so thankful that this is not the end of the story? This life will pass away, but our true home awaits us in heaven. The Bible describes it as a forever-moment beyond the end of time:

> When the perishable has been clothed with the
> imperishable, and the mortal with immortality,
> then the saying that is written will come true:
> "Death has been swallowed up in victory."
>
> 1 CORINTHIANS 15:54

The home that we get the privilege of experiencing here on earth is just a tiny glimpse of heaven, yet that tiny glimpse—experienced in the midst of the pain and suffering of our world—is enough to make us long for the real thing.

We wouldn't long for heaven if we didn't suffer, and heaven wouldn't be a possibility without the suffering of Christ. It's important to drop anchor in the reality that even though loss characterizes our world, no one suffered more loss than Jesus. And because He did, He identifies with our heartbreak and losses. His suffering and His sacrifice made heaven possible for each and every one of us who trusts in Him.

Our suffering points us to His suffering, where we can find joy, peace, and the hope of our eternal home in heaven. He knows how to make every crisis work for our benefit and how to draw us closer to each other and to Him through it. As we grow, we find that all things truly do work together for good (see Romans 8:28), our tears mingle, the pieces of our broken hearts join together like a beautiful stained-glass window, and the light of His love shines through to give us a taste of what awaits us in heaven.

> Peace can be found in the tears of loss when we **remember that we're not home yet**.

26

The moments we think are the end of the story turn out not to be the end, but a new beginning.

PAUL DAVID TRIPP

I HAVE ONLY KNOWN the Cushman family for a short time, but even so, I care about them as if they have been a part of my life for years. We share a common heartbreak and pain through the suffering of our only sons. During a recent event where we were together for a few days, the dad, Kevin, shared some powerful insights on his journey through the dark valley of terminal disease. Here's what he said:

My name is Kevin Cushman, and I am very angry with God! In fact, there have been many times when I hated God. Yes, hated God. My wife, Judy, and I have been married for six years. On December 19, 2010, she gave birth to our first child, Collin. The first several months of Collin's life were rather normal. He ate, slept, and pooped. At around eight months we noticed that Collin wasn't playing or moving as much as he used to. He tired very quickly and spent more time just lying flat on his back. At his nine-month appointment his doctor said it was time to see a specialist and have an MRI done of his brain to see what was going on. On January 6, 2012, after four long months of testing we got the diagnosis. Krabbe leukodystrophy. Life expectancy of thirteen months to two years.

After Collin was diagnosed, nighttime was always difficult. Many nights I would be lucky to get three hours of sleep. The rest of the time was spent holding Collin. This was the time when I would yell at God. I think you can understand my anger and frustration with God. If He was a loving and caring God, how could He allow this to happen? If He was really loving and caring He would fix my son.

What made my anger even more difficult to deal with was the fact that I work with the youth at my church. I would talk about how good God was, but on the inside I was thinking the opposite. I took my anger to the next level during worship. I didn't sing any songs or do any of the responsive readings, and when it came time for Communion, I made sure that I was holding Collin so that he received the blessing and I would just turn and walk away without taking Communion.

This went on for quite some time. My wife always had strong faith, and I secretly looked to her to keep my faith spark going. One day she told me that she thought she was becoming more like me—angry with God—and she felt like turning away from Him too. I knew that I needed to make a change. Not just for her but for me, my daughter, and Collin. I started to work on restoring my faith by asking God for forgiveness, strength, and guidance. . . .

One of the things I would like you to take away from my story is that it's okay to be mad at God. He can take it. But it is equally important to not allow your anger to consume you, like I did. Find someone to talk to that you trust and can be honest with. Ask God for forgiveness. Seek Him. . . . I wish I could tell you that I've been through the valley and have made my way out and my faith is stronger than it's ever been. But honestly, I can't say that. I'm still in the valley. I'm still struggling. But I can say that I am on my way out. I am not there yet, but someday, I will be.

🍃 🍃 🍃

We have all been there, haven't we? Thinking that life should be fair; feeling disappointed and angry with God;

allowing our anger to fester, intensify, and spread, causing more anger and hatred, which always ends up hurting the people we love most. We hope that faith will save the day, but oftentimes it seems to make the journey more difficult.

What I found most encouraging about Kevin's story is the fact that although he is still struggling in the valley, he knows he is not there to stay—he is on his way out. The same goes for you and me. We might not be out of the valley yet, but eventually, and in God's perfect timing, we will be. No matter how long we have to be there, no matter how much pain, anger, suffering, and loss we must endure, the valley is not the end of the story. We will find our way out, and when that day comes, we won't be the same people; we will be changed into His image more perfectly. All that we have had to endure, the heartbreak we have suffered through, and the day-after-day sorrow we have carried will have molded us into the people God longs for us to be.

God will accomplish what He desires in our lives whether we go willingly or kicking and screaming. And regardless of how we think or feel, the truth is,

In all things God works for the good of those who love him, who have been called according to his purpose.
ROMANS 8:28

It might not feel good right now, and your doubts might be casting a shadow over your faith, but God's promises and plans cannot be thwarted. What He says is true—absolutely true, whether or not you believe it. He will work all the circumstances in your life for good.

I love what Job said to God in the midst of his suffering:

I know that you can do all things;
    no purpose of yours can be thwarted.
You asked, "Who is this that obscures my plans
      without knowledge?"
    Surely I spoke of things I did not understand,
    things too wonderful for me to know.

You said, "Listen now, and I will speak;
    I will question you,
    and you shall answer me."
My ears had heard of you
    but now my eyes have seen you.
Therefore I despise myself
    and repent in dust and ashes.
JOB 42:2-6

After all the loss and suffering Job went through, he came to a clearer understanding of who God is, and as a result he was moved to repent and seek forgiveness for thinking he knew better than God. What a response from someone who had spent a long time in the valley.

Whether you are just trying to survive in a deep valley or thriving upon a mountaintop, God is not finished with you yet. If you're still breathing, there is more to your life story. "This," whatever it is, is not the end. And while you live your days one moment at a time, regardless of your circumstances, I hope and pray you will remember that your pain is not in vain, your tears matter, and God will work it all together for your good and His glory.

He who began a good work in you will carry it on to completion until the day of Christ Jesus.

PHILIPPIANS 1:6

Peace in the midst of loss comes when we **remember that the valleys are part of the journey,** not the end of the story.

27

This is where my comeback starts. I won't have any
more time to fear and worry or ask God why . . .
because I'll be too busy praising Him.

UNKNOWN

THERE HAVE BEEN MANY "FIRSTS" in my faith journey. After
I became a Christian in the fall of 1998, one of the first
things I did in response to my newfound faith in Christ was
buy a cross necklace. This was simply an outward expression
of an inward change in my heart. The cross had always been
symbolic, but suddenly it held deep meaning and eternal
hope. After I bought the cross necklace, my next stop was
our local Christian bookstore, where I purchased my first
car decal—a shiny silver Christian fish symbol that found
a home on the back of my black Chevy Suburban. Again,
it was an outward symbol of an inward change. However,
this outward sign did more than reflect my faith; it also kept
me accountable while driving. *Allegedly*, I might have had
a lead foot on very rare occasions.

I was so excited about Jesus that I kept the momentum going by following up my shiny fish with a Bible, a 365-day devotional, a highly recommended Max Lucado book, a Beth Moore Bible study, and a "Jesus Rocks" T-shirt. I was on a roll. Whatever I could buy, read, wear, or do in order to learn more about and express my faith, I was all in.

Looking back, I can't help but laugh. Jim thought I was losing it. The kids went along with it—probably because they were young and didn't have a choice. My mother was right there with me, soul hungry for anything related to God, healing, and hope. It was the beginning of the most incredible, life-altering journey—a journey I am still on to this day.

One of the most foundational changes that took place early on in my walk with God was my practice of thanksgiving and praise. Before I came to faith in Christ I had no idea what it meant to praise God, and unfortunately, I was not a very thankful person. Honestly, I do not believe any of us has the heart to be thankful or sincerely praise God unless we know Him. Unless Christ intervenes in our lives, we are hardwired by sin to be selfish and narcissistic, driven to pursue dreams rooted in personal gain and jaded motives.

We cannot choose to live any other way. Unless Christ occupies the throne of our hearts, we will always choose self over sacrifice, greed over gratitude, and the temptations of this world over the glory of God. It's the path of least resistance, and sadly, it comes naturally! That being said, when you come face-to-face with your need for a Savior, and you choose, by faith, to seek forgiveness and new life through Him, everything changes. And I mean *everything*!

As a result of God opening my heart to know and love Him, I now long to live a life characterized by gratitude and praise. In fact, I think thanksgiving and praise walk hand in hand throughout our faith journey. The Psalms encourage us to live with an "attitude of gratitude." For example, Psalm 100:4 says to

> Enter his gates with thanksgiving
> and his courts with praise;
> give thanks to him and praise his name.

In Psalm 69:30 the psalmist proclaims,

> I will praise God's name in song
> and glorify him with thanksgiving.

The New Testament also mentions the importance of thanksgiving and praise. This is one of my favorite verses:

> Do not be anxious about anything, but in
> every situation, by prayer and petition, with
> thanksgiving, present your requests to God.
> And the peace of God, which transcends all
> understanding, will guard your hearts and your
> minds in Christ Jesus.
> PHILIPPIANS 4:6-7

After I typed that last verse, I thought back to the story of Job we looked at on day 2. After he was told that all his children had died, he humbly trusted God even though he was completely devastated, saying, "Naked I came from my mother's womb, and naked I will depart. The LORD gave and the LORD has taken away; may the name of the LORD be praised" (Job 1:21).

Honestly, the first time I read Job's response, I thought, *Well, he's clearly crazy, and I would never be able to respond to loss like he did!* However, the more I draw near to God, the more I love Him, and the more I appreciate and respect Job's humble response. He's right! The Lord gives and He takes away and regardless of how we feel about either, He's God. And whether we understand or agree with His decisions or not, He is worthy of our praise.

Whether you are overwhelmed with loss or buried beneath the weight of life's various trials, thanksgiving and praise will bring you peace. Peace about your questions and emotions, your self-will and circumstances, your pain, and anything else that may get between you and God.

In a very practical sense, when you move your focus away from the pain and praise Him instead, peace is unleashed. And that's because peace is not an end in itself; it's a byproduct, a result of keeping God on the throne of your heart. Circumstances will try to drive a wedge between you and the One who loves you more than anyone ever could. But when you choose to be thankful and praise God regardless of your circumstances or how you feel in the midst of them, you are changed.

Of course this is not easy. But that shouldn't come as a surprise: If it's worth a lot, it's going to cost a lot. You must be intentional, because being sincerely thankful is an act of the will, not an emotional response.

When I find myself wallowing in doubt, sorrow, fear, self-pity, or any of the other real human emotions we experience as a result of heartbreak or loss, I allow myself to be authentic and express exactly what I am feeling in the moment. And then I choose to refocus! I choose Jesus. I purposefully tune out the chatter of the world and turn on music or messages that will uplift my soul. I don't ignore my feelings or pretend they do not exist, but I do not allow them to overcome me.

We intentionally choose to focus on God not for the purpose of changing our circumstances. Instead, with thankful hearts committed to praising God, we can trust that He, in His sovereign power, will use our circumstances to change us.

Peace in the face of loss can be found when, despite how we feel and regardless of the cost, we **choose to give thanks and praise to God**.

28

LORD, remind me how brief my time on earth will be. Remind me that my days are numbered— how fleeting my life is.

PSALM 39:4, NLT

WHENEVER I MISS HUNTER, which is daily, I remind myself that every day I am closer to heaven. For me, this knowledge is profoundly comforting. And even though the pain of missing Hunter persists, being one day closer to seeing him face-to-face encourages me. It motivates me to anchor my heart more steadfastly in the love and loyalty of God.

I value the gift of life and do not take it for granted, yet my longing to be with Hunter and Jesus gives me an eternal perspective that keeps my heart and mind tethered to a heavenly reality. The wound I have as a result of Hunter's death is still raw, even after eleven years, but it helps keep me focused on eternal priorities, and it also helps me to be unjaded in my relationship with God.

Although today I am one day closer to seeing Hunter

again, I will never know how close I really am. But God does. And I imagine that we are all much closer than we think.

Life is not a roll of the dice from the next moment to the next day or decade. It is intricately designed by a Master Architect who orchestrates every detail, working all things together for a greater purpose and glory. We all tend to live with the misguided conviction that our next breath is simply a matter of inhaling and exhaling. Though it is daunting from this side of eternity, the reality is that tomorrow is not promised to any of us—and, in fact, neither is the next heartbeat.

This truth reminds me of some powerful verses in 2 Corinthians, where the apostle Paul was encouraging believers to focus on the end result rather than on the temporary pain they experienced through life's trials. He wrote:

> Therefore we do not lose heart. Though outwardly we are wasting away, yet inwardly we are being renewed day by day. For our light and momentary troubles are achieving for us an eternal glory that far outweighs them all. So we fix our eyes not on what is seen, but on what is unseen, since what is seen is temporary, but what is unseen is eternal.
>
> 2 CORINTHIANS 4:16-18

It's a daily challenge to keep our eyes on eternity—to trust that what is unseen now will last longer than anything we can currently see or touch. This quote from author Morgan Matson speaks to the struggle: "A thousand moments that I had just taken for granted—mostly because I had assumed that there would be a thousand more."[6] I hate to admit it, but I used to assume that tomorrow was a given, and I took for granted the gift of each day. Maybe it was because I was young and naive and expected my heart to keep beating well into hundreds of tomorrows. For most of my life, I did not know what the Bible said about death, nor did I appreciate the brevity of life. The depth of this reality did not take root in my soul . . . until Hunter.

As my family and I watched Hunter struggle to live one day at a time, God taught us how to truly *live*, fixing our eyes, just as Paul did, on what is unseen, and humbly numbering our days. Although outwardly we witnessed Hunter suffer and waste away, inwardly we were being renewed day by day, given a greater appreciation for life both here in time and for eternity. For the brief eight and a half years that Hunter was alive, our entire family and those who knew and loved him drew strength from his weakness, found their voice in his silence, and discovered the meaning of living through his terminal illness.

If death on earth were not a reality, what would inspire us to value the gift of every breath? What would cause us to hope for a reality beyond time? We all have a shelf life bound by an unknown expiration date—a timeline that ends exactly when it is meant to. Every one of us has the same unrenewable resource: time. Psalm 31:15 assures us that our times are in God's hands; He has determined all our moments and prepared us to step into them as they await us.

Jim's battle with cancer was another poignant reminder to live fully with the limited time we have left. Not for selfish gain or the pleasures of this world, and not even to do good, altruistic works—but to glorify God. To live for Him, rather than ourselves, is to truly live!

🍃 🍃 🍃

Life is temporary, with each sunset bringing us one day closer to forever. Let this be a reminder for all of us to number our days, appreciate each one, and fill them with eternal pursuits that reflect a heart focused on God. And as we grow more mindful, every day realizing that we are never more than a breath away from our forever home, we will find peace in the knowledge that we're just passing through. A peace that surpasses all understanding and allows us to fix our affections on the unseen while making every moment in the here and now matter.

James 4:14 drives this idea home with a serious reality check: "Why, you do not even know what will happen tomorrow. What is your life? You are a mist that appears for a little while and then vanishes." Jim Elliot, the missionary whose life was taken by the spears of the Auca Indians, might have been inspired by those words when he wrote: "Wherever you are, *be all there*. Live to the hilt every situation you believe to be the will of God."[7] Let's be inspired to change the way we live, determining to walk through time with eternity in mind. For the moment is coming when the sun will go down, but we won't be one day closer . . . we'll be there.

> Peace comes when we **fix our eyes on the eternal** while choosing to *live* fully in the present.

29

We cannot tell what may happen to us in the strange medley of life. But we can decide what happens in us—how we take it, what we do with it—and that is what really counts in the end.

JOSEPH FORT NEWTON

"MRSA IS GOING TO HAVE TO WAIT!"

I can still hear Jim's resolute voice abounding with determination. He was gearing up to go on a hunting trip in New Zealand with our nephew Zac, and it promised to be a once-in-a-lifetime experience.

After Jim's second oral cancer diagnosis, his treatment regimen included chemotherapy and radiation. Due to the fact that his cancer had spread to a rather dangerous area near his brain, surgery was not an option. The only option we were given, even with a second opinion, was chemo and radiation—so that's exactly what Jim did. Three rounds of chemotherapy and a daunting forty-two rounds of radiation. If you know someone who has had this type of treatment, you know that the effects linger long after the cancer is gone, and the fallout can be significant.

While Jim was still getting treatments he contracted MRSA, also known as methicillin-resistant Staphylococcus aureus, or the "super bug." MRSA is a bacterium that can be very dangerous, even life-threatening, causing infections all over the body. It is highly contagious and difficult to treat because it is resistant to most of the common antibiotics.[8] Jim had to go on two powerful IV antibiotics for an overwhelming six-week run.

This was the "colorful" backdrop to Zac and Jim's pending international hunting expedition to New Zealand, which had been planned before Jim was diagnosed with cancer a second time. Because of the complexity of hunting in other countries, the trip had to be booked an entire year in advance. And as soon as the hunting logistics had been nailed down and all the other traveling details were set in motion, pursuing the mighty New Zealand stag was all Jim and Zac talked about.

For months they had been preparing, joyfully obsessing over their imminent excursion. But in the midst of all the fun and excitement, cancer decided to rear its ugly head again with a vengeance—and then MRSA as well. Clearly, sickness and disease don't care much about the plans people make or the lives they hope to live. Unfortunately, it seemed that the much-anticipated hunting trip would have to wait.

And wait it did. But after Jim had completed his chemo and radiation treatments and recovered from MRSA, the boys were ready to roll once again. Talk of New Zealand, red stags, and the amazing trip they would soon embark on continued to echo through the halls of the Kelly household. A week before their scheduled flight, however, Jim started feeling uncharacteristically weak and lethargic. We knew his body was still in recovery mode from the intense cancer treatments, but this seemed especially irregular, so he went to see his physician.

MRSA again. When we heard the news I thought for sure that Jim would be devastated. And he was initially, but it didn't take long for his fierce resolve to overcome his diagnosis. After prayer and a few hours of talking it all through, his response was classic Jim Kelly—"MRSA is going to have to wait!" He simply was not going to allow the virus to steal from him again. Jim was bound and determined to take his nephew hunting, and that's exactly what he did.

Of course I was apprehensive about the entire situation. First of all, traveling across the globe after he was just told that he had MRSA did not seem very wise. In addition, Jim was still trying to get stronger after all the cancer treatments— and this trip would be physically demanding. To say that I thought he was crazy would be an understatement—and yet, his kind of crazy turned out to be a determination to *live* life like I have never seen.

Jim and Zac went to New Zealand, and today the memory book bursting with amazing photos sits on display at our lodge. Oddly, and I would even say miraculously, the MRSA went away as mysteriously as it appeared. It didn't just "wait" like Jim proclaimed it would have to; it literally disappeared.

The greatest blessing in this situation really wasn't the hunting trip or the time Jim and Zac were able to spend together—although these were tremendous blessings. It wasn't even the fact that the MRSA mysteriously went away—even though that was certainly a blessing from God. I believe the greatest blessing was Jim's raw determination against the dreadful infection that stood Goliath-like in his path. By faith, he made a decision to live rather than let a diagnosis intimidate him. He was not going to allow MRSA—or anything else, for that matter—to keep him from spending time with his nephew.

The epic saga of David and Goliath is filled with high drama, intrigue, and passion for God as a teenage boy stands up against a mighty, nine-foot-tall, seasoned warrior, replete with armor and weaponry. The thought of this brave young man who dared defy the fierce giant glaring down at him inspires and encourages me—especially because David loved God with all his heart and was willing to serve Him despite the cost to himself. David told Goliath,

> All those gathered here will know that it is not by sword or spear that the LORD saves; for the battle is the LORD's, and he will give all of you into our hands.
>
> 1 SAMUEL 17:47

By faith, he looked beyond the dire circumstances with his evil adversary and, instead, wholeheartedly trusted the God he loved. And we all know how that ended!

Similarly, Jim was conviction driven and full of faith as he took his stand against the giant blocking his path—MRSA. And we know how that ended too.

Maybe you are facing your own unique giant right now. Perhaps it's a financial struggle, a troubling family situation, a problem in your workplace, or a recent cancer diagnosis for you or someone you love. Whatever it is, however scary and intimidating it might be, it's not bigger than Jesus. Goliath was bigger and stronger than David, but he was not bigger or stronger than David's God. MRSA was bigger than Jim, but it could not contend with God. Don't be intimidated by what you see. Instead, have confidence in the One whom you cannot see, for in the midst of all that you are going through, He is there. Remember, Hebrews 11:1 assures us,

Now faith is being sure of what we hope for and certain of what we do not see.

Our God is mighty to save and takes great delight in rescuing His children. God is for you, not against you. Whatever your giants are, God is greater. If you don't believe me, ask David or Jim!

Peace can be found when we **trust that God is greater than all our fears**.

30

*This is a thing many people outside your grief
cannot understand: that you have not simply lost
one person, at one point in time. You have lost their
presence in every aspect of your life. Your future
has changed as well as your "now."*

MEGAN DEVINE

I WAS SOUND ASLEEP when the doors on the fireplace in our bedroom started banging. Usually their rhythmic cadence begins when there's a storm outside. It was early, so I rolled over and was trying to doze back off when the wind howled through the bedroom again, causing the pocket door leading into the office to bang along with the fireplace doors.

The crashing of doors and blowing of the wind grew stronger, sabotaging all my efforts to try to get more sleep. The storm outside took me from the cozy comforts of bed to the big picture window facing our backyard. As I pulled back the curtains, another strong gust of wind howled through the fireplace. I looked outside to find dark skies, a torrential downpour, swaying trees, and rain hammering the windows so hard that it seemed they might even shatter.

As I stood there watching the storm, the first thought that ran through my mind was *God is crying with me today*. It was Hunter's heaven anniversary. Eleven years ago, on August 5, 2005, Hunter's life and suffering here on earth ended and he began his forever journey with God in heaven. And even though I know where Hunter is, this day is always hard.

Just as abruptly as the storm came raging in, it was gone. And as I stood there looking out the window, I wept and watched in awe as the sun pushed through the murky, ominous clouds and the rain and howling winds ceased. The dark faded from the sky, our backyard birds went about their business, and just like that—the storm was gone and the sun was shining. It all happened in a matter of minutes, and yet its significance continued to penetrate my soul, reminding me that although weeping may endure for a night (or on and off for eleven years), joy comes in the morning (see Psalm 30:5).

After I walked away from the window and the awe of the moment, I grabbed my journal and penned the following . . .

Heavenly Father—Thank You for waking me up this morning to tears from heaven. Thank You for knowing the depth of my pain and crying with me, assuring me that it's okay to weep, even eleven years later. I cannot believe it has been that long—eleven

*years. It seems like forever and yet hurts as if it
happened yesterday. So much has changed. Every
day is hard and yet we keep on living. Some days I
actually feel fully alive, but I never forget.*

*Lord, as quickly as the tears from heaven
came—they were gone. And with the brilliance and
warmth of the sun came an overwhelming peace
and assurance, a comfort that I desperately needed to
wake up to today, on this day—August 5th, 2016.
The comfort of knowing that although everything
has changed and continues to change—YOU stay the
same. YOU remain constant and true.*

*Thank You for getting me out of bed and starting
my day with Your presence and a clear reminder that
You share in my sorrows. . . . You cry with me because
You know the depths of my anguish. You see me and
meet me right where I am. You hold me and guide me
from heartbreak and grief to healing and hope. You
open my heart and mind and remind me that joy is
coming. It's coming! Hunter is in my future! But even
more than that amazing truth is the fact that You are
my right now and my forever.*

*You weep with me in the present and remind me
that joy is coming. Thank You, Lord, for this day
and the gift of moments and memories. Thank You
for allowing me to reflect on all that was and all that
will be . . . on our amazing life with Hunter and our
forever life with both of you. Sometimes I don't want*

to move. I don't want to continue with the rest of the day. I just want to sit here with my Hunter memories. But I can't do that. Thank You for helping me to carry on . . . one moment and one memory at a time.

🍃 🍃 🍃

Maybe for you, it has only been a few weeks, a few days, or a few hours. Maybe it's been a month, or a year, or even a decade. But no matter how long it has been since you took the hit that brought about the pain you are feeling, every moment matters to God. Every tear matters to the Almighty, and He is tender to those who hurt. The Bible says,

> The Lord is close to the brokenhearted
>   and saves those who are crushed in spirit.
> PSALM 34:18

When God is involved, everything has purpose and meaning. And although we live in a world that is constantly changing from one moment to the next, like the storm outside my window, God never changes. He is the rock-solid, unchanging, strong foundation upon which everything in life exists. He's not going anywhere. His steadfast love, mercy, and grace will endure.

This is how you survive and, dare I say, thrive: by trusting in and depending upon the unshakable, unchanging nature and perfect promises of God. I love how A.W. Tozer describes this:

What peace it brings to the Christian's heart to realize that our Heavenly Father never differs from Himself. In coming to Him at any time we need not wonder whether we shall find Him in a receptive mood. He is always receptive to misery and need, as well as to love and faith. He does not keep office hours nor set aside periods when He will see no one. Neither does He change His mind about anything. Today, this moment, He feels towards His creatures, toward babies, toward the sick, the fallen, the sinful, exactly as He did when He sent His only-begotten Son into the world to die for mankind.[9]

Or, as the writer to the Hebrews put it:

Jesus Christ is the same yesterday and today and forever.
HEBREWS 13:8

As Billy Graham once said, "From one end of the Bible to the other, God assures us that He will never go back on His promises."[10] Let's not waste one more breath thinking about yesterday or worrying and fretting about tomorrow. Focus on this moment, this day, as gifts from a God who never changes, who is always present and forever faithful.

Peace in the face of loss comes when we remember that although everything else in life changes, **God never changes**.

31

God is our refuge and strength,
an ever-present help in trouble.

PSALM 46:1

WHEN I CHECKED MY E-MAILS EARLIER, I saw a message
from my dear friend Kathleen. Usually when she sends an
e-mail it's not good news, and today was no different. She
was writing to let me know that a child with Krabbe disease,
an adorable one-year-old boy named Charles, had died. Just
two days earlier, Kathleen had messaged me about another
little boy—a two-year-old named Max. He, too, died from
Krabbe disease.

Kathleen knows about these children and their families
because she is the director of family care for the Hunter's
Hope Foundation, the organization that Jim and I established to help children and families suffering from leuko-
dystrophies after Hunter was diagnosed with Krabbe
disease. Kathleen doesn't just know the children and their

families; she identifies with their heartache because she, too, has a beautiful daughter in heaven. Her precious Jacquelyn was just five months shy of her fifth birthday when she breathed her last.

Unfortunately, e-mails like this from Kathleen are nothing new, and yet I'm always shocked when I hear about the loss of yet another child. And as harsh as it might sound, in our foundation work we deal with death on a frequent basis, becoming intimately involved with some of the most heartrending experiences you can imagine. Sometimes there seems to be no end to the tears. Yet, though it is agonizing at times, comforting the broken and hurting is what we do.

It's certainly not what I would have chosen, but I thank God that because of Hunter's life and the comfort He has given us, we are equipped to comfort others. That being said, it is never easy. In addition to experiencing sorrow for another family's loss, every time I hear the dreadful news that another child has been diagnosed or died from disease, to a certain degree I experience the loss of my Hunter all over again. I weep and mourn and feel that same deep brokenness, sorrow, and emptiness that overwhelmed me when God called him home.

Sometimes when I receive messages from Kathleen, I just cry and ask God, *"Why?"* Regardless of the measure of faith I have in these moments, a loss is still a loss and the pain still hurts. And even though I know that the pain wouldn't go away even if God were to explain why, I still ask anyway because I find comfort and peace in asking Him the hard questions. There are no easy answers, but given the intensity of the heartbreak, if I didn't pour my heart out to God, I would be lost. We all need an outlet for our pain, doubt, fear, anger, sorrow, and all the other emotions that make us who we are. When we keep all the hurt inside, we only end up hurting even more.

In the midst of trying to process the death of these precious little children, I think about their parents and siblings, along with all their extended family members and loved ones—and I grieve for them, as well. I don't know their hearts, but I can certainly relate to their pain.

Most of the families we have the privilege of ministering to through our foundation are mad at God—and I don't blame them. Anger is a normal response to loss, deep hurt, and a sense of injustice. It's a vital part of the grief process. If you're going to be angry at someone for your loss, God is the only One fully capable of handling it and loving you at the same time. He's also the only One who knows you well enough to perfectly help you deal with your emotions. In His sovereignty, He created us with the capacity to respond to life's tragedies as well as triumphs. Denying anger its rightful place in the grieving and healing process will only hurt you and everyone you love even more.

🌿 🌿 🌿

Since the creation of our foundation, I have had numerous grief-stricken family members come to me with tear-filled eyes, questioning, "Why would God allow this to happen to a child?" And even though I'm much more comfortable giving hugs than answers, I respond the same way to everyone who has asked me this daunting question: "I don't know why, but I choose to trust God anyway because I know that He knows. No, it doesn't make it any easier, but at least I have somewhere to go with my pain."

That's what we all need, isn't it—a place to go with our pain? We need a refuge in which to weather the fierce storms of trauma and heartache—a safe haven where we can be vulnerable and find shelter for our fears, tears, and broken hearts. Imagine if you had to keep your sorrow and anger hidden deep inside of you. Trust me—you could not survive. Isolation in the midst of loss is deadly. We need God and each other to survive, and to eventually thrive again.

We need to let God do what only He can do—bind up the brokenhearted. When Jesus read Scripture at a synagogue in Nazareth, he chose a passage from Isaiah:

> The Spirit of the Sovereign LORD is on me,
> because the LORD has anointed me
> to proclaim good news to the poor.
> He has sent me to bind up the brokenhearted,
> to proclaim freedom for the captives
> and release from darkness for the prisoners.

ISAIAH 61:1

You may feel imprisoned by the darkness of your anger, paralyzed by sorrow, destitute of any of the treasures your dreams once held, and afraid to move forward with your life. Don't despair; you're only a prayer away from receiving the peace and comfort you desperately need. Isaiah 41:13 is one of my favorite verses, and I hope it encourages you:

> For I am the LORD your God
>   who takes hold of your right hand
> and says to you, Do not fear;
>   I will help you.

> Peace in the depths of loss is found when we **allow God to be our refuge** as we experience all the emotions of grief.

32

My faith rests not in what I am, or shall be, or feel, or know, but in what Christ is, in what He has done, and in what He is now doing for me.

CHARLES SPURGEON

WHEN I FIRST MET and eventually started dating the icon who would become my husband, he was at the height of his celebrated professional football career. As quarterback of the Buffalo Bills, he had already led his team to two consecutive Super Bowl appearances. Jim was (and still is) a local and national sports celebrity. No matter where we go, including foreign countries, at least one person will recognize him and ask for a photo, autograph, or handshake. I have watched Jim interact with fans for years and continue to be amazed by how a simple greeting can change someone's entire day.

As you can imagine, I had no idea what I was getting myself into when I met Jim. At the time I was twenty-one years old and very naive. I had just graduated from college with a business degree, and I was confidently pursuing my dreams. I was driven by passion and boundless expectations, and dating and eventually marrying a celebrity athlete was not on my radar screen. After I met Jim, however, it didn't take long for me to get caught up in the narcissistic celebrity lifestyle. Suddenly I was cool by association, someone people wanted to know because I was with an NFL powerhouse at the top of his game. You can try all you want to remain humble and grounded when you have the treasures of this world at your fingertips, but it's nearly impossible.

I fell willingly for all the glitz and glamour that came with being on Jim's arm. At first I was "Jim Kelly's girlfriend," but that changed three years later when Jim asked me to marry him. At that point I was no longer the girlfriend but "Jim Kelly's fiancée." I was a fast learner and instinctively knew who and what I had to be as the fiancée of one of the biggest names on ESPN.

Of course, you know how the story unfolded. The exciting and well-publicized engagement blossomed into a full-fledged fairy-tale wedding a year later, leading me to become "Jim Kelly's wife."

After our firstborn, Erin Marie, was born, I became "Mommie"—and what an awe-inspiring honor and blessing it was (and still is) to be known by that name. Its significance, which swiftly enveloped so much of my identity, became sharper as my second child, Hunter, found his place on the "Team Kelly" roster. Becoming "Hunter's mom," with the astounding blessings and privileges unique to that role, unexpectedly enriched and changed my life beyond comprehension.

My daughters have also had to wrestle with living in the shadow of a life label to a certain degree because they're often introduced as "Jim Kelly's daughters." Of course, this isn't such a bad thing when you're trying to get good seats for a Justin Bieber concert. And don't misunderstand me—there's nothing wrong with the label unless you allow it to become your identity and define who you are.

My identity has been wrapped up in many life labels: Jim Kelly's wife, a mother, a mother who lost a child, a CEO, an author, and a speaker. All the different labels identify unique facets of the whole—they are the many "whats" that clarify aspects of "who" Jill Kelly is. No identity has defined me more than being Hunter's mom. And when he went to heaven, I lost more than my son; I lost part of myself.

Hunter's life had consumed me. Everything I did or did not do revolved around Hunter as if he were the axis my world turned on. He needed around-the-clock care that demanded my time and everything else I had to give. For the first year and a half after Hunter was diagnosed, I barely left the house, and if I did, all I could think about was getting back home. In so many ways that was a beautiful thing. Hunter taught me more about life than anyone I have ever met. He made me want to be a better person. He inspired me to live the kind of life that impacts people because that's exactly what he did. And the ripple effect of his life is still alive and well, changing others' lives on a daily basis.

But because my identity and my life were so intertwined

with Hunter's, after he went to heaven, I completely lost sight of who I was. This can happen to us as a result of all sorts of losses we experience throughout our lives. The loss of a job or career, the loss of the ability to do what we have always done, the loss of financial security, a divorce, the death of a child—and on and on the list goes.

Regardless of the life labels we have allowed to define who we are, we have one true identity: the person God hardwired us to be. We are not defined by what we do for a living, who we are married to, how much money we make, the losses we have endured, or any of the other things the world tries to label us with. Those are all variations on things we do or what we have gone through, but they're not who we truly are. When we confuse the two, we tend to compromise the truth.

We were created by God and for God, and until we understand this foundational truth, life and the losses we endure will never make sense. Our identity and value are found in Christ alone, not in the life labels other people hang on us (or we hang on ourselves).

Your loss does not define you. The circumstances that have transpired in order to bring you to this season in your life do not define you. You are defined by your identity as a beloved child of God. First John 3:1 says:

> See what great love the Father has lavished on us,
> that we should be called children of God! And that
> is what we are!

Child of God is the greatest and truest label we can ever have.

Our losses do not strip us of our identity any more than our gains or victories add to it. We are who God made us to be, and that alone is what defines us. Above all else, the only way for us to know who we are is to know our Creator. To know Him is to know the truth, and in that truth we discover who we are. And that changes everything.

Peace in the face of loss comes when we **find our true identity** in who God created us to be.

33

Blessed is the one who perseveres under trial because,
having stood the test, that person will receive
the crown of life that the Lord has promised
to those who love him.

JAMES 1:12

WHEN I AM WRITING, I try to cloister myself with the Lord as much as possible in an effort to clear my head and heart before Him. For that reason, while I am quiet with God and attached to my laptop, it is rare for me to venture out and check my website e-mail account. However, the other day, I found myself reading a message sent by a mom of young children (with another baby on the way) and felt led to share it with you.

> Hi, Jill,
>
> About a month ago my husband came home and shocked me with the news that he didn't think he wanted to be married anymore. . . .

I am devastated. Devastated that the baby in my womb is not bonding with her father.

Devastated that my kids pray for their daddy to come home each night.

I'm so scared about raising these three kids on my own. It feels so daunting. I'm tired and short tempered but I am trying to have faith and be strong. What do you do when you feel so hopeless and overwhelmed? I just feel lost. I got married to be married through thick and thin. I thought we would stand by each other and work it out. He won't even try. I feel like I'm sinking.

My heart hurts so much. I am trying to remember that the Lord is working for good, but this is so hard. If you have any advice, I would love to hear it. Thank you for taking the time to listen.

After I read this message, I wanted to hug her and her children. I could not just sit there. I had to do something, so I left my laptop, got up, and went outside, just to breathe. My heart was overwhelmed, and I could not help but think about those three beautiful, innocent children and their confusion, pain, and sense of loss. All of it caused by the one person who was supposed to protect, love, and care for them no matter what—their father. Was he really willing to selfishly walk away just because he supposedly fell out of love with their mother? Did he even understand what true, unconditional love was? Did he fathom that we all fall short of one another's expectations? In fact, I've heard it said that expectation is the root of all heartache. I believe this to be true—unless, of course, your expectations are in Christ alone. But what about the promises he made, the vows that unified them as one—"in sickness and health, until death do us part"?

As I prayed and pondered all these things, the Lord reminded me of what He had said in the Gospel of John:

I have told you all this so that you may have peace in me. Here on earth you will have many trials and sorrows. But take heart, because I have overcome the world.

JOHN 16:33, NLT

Here on earth we *will* have many trials and sorrows.

Because of experience, we know this to be true—but it still hurts. Sometimes the pain is so deep that we forget the greater truth: that in the midst of our trials, we have Jesus—who has overcome. This is how we overcome as well.

The apostle Peter confirmed Jesus' words about trials when he proclaimed,

In this you greatly rejoice, though now for a little while you may have had to suffer grief in all kinds of trials. These have come so that your faith—of greater worth than gold, which perishes even though refined by fire—may be proved genuine and may result in praise, glory and honor when Jesus Christ is revealed.

I PETER 1:6-7

Although it doesn't take away the pain, knowing that our trials come to prove our faith genuine is encouraging. Why? Well, don't you want to know that your faith is real? I want to know beyond any shadow of doubt that the God I profess to believe in and trust is who He says He is. And as a result of knowing who He is, I know who I am. I also want to know that my trials and tears count for something. Pain without purpose is a waste, but in God's Kingdom our struggles are never wasted.

But how can we rejoice through our trials, as Peter witnessed his contemporaries doing? We can rejoice by remembering that Jesus overcame and has promised to comfort and take care of us in the midst of our pain. We don't have joy because of the trial, but because of *Jesus in the midst* of the trial. He helps us overcome!

With all these verses in mind, I eventually wandered back home, sat down in front of my laptop, and responded to the e-mail . . .

I am literally crying with you right now . . . RIGHT NOW, crying. I do not understand why—and my initial response is to get really mad at your husband. But I know what anger can do and it is not good, not good at all. So instead I choose trust over understanding . . . God over doubt . . . and to breathe when I want to stop breathing. . . .

The good that we think God is working together with all of our pain does not always feel good, and most of the time it does not end up being the kind of good we had hoped for based upon what we believe. But God is always good, and if He has allowed a torrential downpour of pain into your life and the lives of your sweet, innocent children, He will supply every need you have in the midst of it. He will be your shelter, calming the wind and waves when the time is right. Of course my heart breaks even more for the children, and yet I have to remind myself that God loves them more than you ever could. His plan for their lives will not be thwarted because of the choices their daddy is making. God is their heavenly Father and yours. He is enough. . . . God can do the IMPOSSIBLE. Focus on Him. Let Him do what only He can do.

What trials are you facing today? No matter what your circumstances are, cling to the truth that they are not a surprise to God. Although we may not see it now, He has overcome them all. We can overcome through Him.

Peace in the shock of loss comes when we remember that because Christ has overcome on our behalf, **we, too, can overcome through Him**.

34

*A year from now you will wish
you had started today.*

KAREN LAMB

So far in this devotional we've spent a lot of time talking about the emotional and spiritual aspects of grieving. But we're not only emotional and spiritual beings; we're also physical beings, and the way we treat our bodies has a significant effect on how we feel. In this devotion I want to talk about one of the practical tools I've found that has helped me deal with the painful emotions that can come with loss. Eight months after my son, Hunter, died, I penned this journal entry:

April 17, 2006—I don't understand what's going on. I woke up this morning oppressed by a heaviness of heart I'm not familiar with. HELP ME! I'm scared to death. What is this? I feel like I've fallen into a dark abyss of depression and despair. Lord, where are You? Why do I feel so alone, abandoned? Never in all my life have I felt so downcast, so afraid, so lifeless. . . . My thoughts and fears overwhelm me day and night. . . .

Do You see me? Do You hear me? Please rescue me from this battle waged against me. . . . I need help! Is this "the valley of the shadow of death"? My God, deliver me from this torment.

Sleep eluded me, and food had no taste. Within two weeks I had lost twenty pounds. The bold green irises of my eyes were fading to gray. With each passing day the immensity of dread and desperation grew. It got to the point where, a few times, I felt as if I would literally die from suffocation. I spent hours balled up on the floor in my closet, praying with my face buried in my Bible. . . .

Weeks passed. I continued to descend deeper into dread and what I feared was madness. Finally, we sought medical intervention in addition to the intense prayers I was already receiving.[11]

Other than Hunter's diagnosis and Jim's cancer battle, what I just shared with you was one of the scariest seasons in my life. Though unseen and not physical, both depression and anxiety are as real as a broken bone and can be triggered by a broken heart following loss. I did not understand how debilitating depression and anxiety can be until I walked through that valley myself. Now I know.

In addition to prayer and medical intervention, one more intervention helped me significantly during the darkest days of my grief journey: exercise. I cannot help but laugh right now as I wonder what you are thinking. *Exercise? Really?* If you are anything like me, you probably have a love/hate relationship with sweating. Some days you love it, but most days you hate it. And now I am laughing even more since lately the sweating I have been doing has absolutely nothing to do with exercise and everything to do with premenopause. Can I get an "Amen!" or a "Lord help us"?

My relationship with God, prayer, and Bible study have been by far the most significant components helping me find true peace and authentic joy in the midst of loss. However, after these three vital disciplines, exercise has impacted my life more than anything else. I know, I know—it sounds almost ridiculous, doesn't it? Well, it's not.

I am not a personal trainer or nutritionist, so clearly I am not equipped to tell you exactly what your body needs and why. But what I can tell you with 100 percent certainty is this: If you are going through a season of loss right now, getting some form of exercise *will* help you.

A few minutes spent searching the Internet can dispel any doubts about the positive impact exercise has on those suffering loss, trauma, depression, or anxiety. The experts who have weighed in on this topic are featured in marquee publications such as the *New York Times*, *Psychology Today*, and the *Huffington Post*, on renowned medical websites including WebMD and the Mayo Clinic, and even in articles from Harvard Medical School and the University of Maryland Medical Center. (A quick word of wisdom, from someone who has overindulged to a fault: Be prayerful and careful regarding medical information obtained from the Internet. I have learned that too much information can sometimes be just as harmful as no information. So investigate with caution.)

An article from Mayo Clinic staff states categorically that "the links between anxiety, depression and exercise aren't entirely clear—but working out and other forms of physical activity can definitely ease symptoms of anxiety or depression and make you feel better. Exercise may also help keep anxiety and depression from coming back once you're feeling better."[12] And while the article goes into some detail about the medical and psychological benefits of exercise, my experience might speak to the issue more persuasively than even the experts do.

In 1 Corinthians 6:19-20, the Bible emphatically admonishes us to honor God with our bodies, saying,

Do you not know that your bodies are temples of the Holy Spirit, who is in you, whom you have received from God? You are not your own; you were bought at a price. Therefore honor God with your bodies.

Certainly this verse speaks to many things—including avoiding immoral or unhealthy activities that will harm us—but it also encompasses exercise and taking care of the one body God has given us. When I was in the throes of intense loss and sorrow, this Scripture motivated me to honor God by exercising, which ultimately helped get my heart and head back in a right relationship with the Lord—and everyone else, for that matter.

The day I sat down to write this, I experienced an onslaught of trouble, one incident after another. The tension was thick, and the air seemed to be getting thinner by the moment. My oldest daughter, Erin, could tell that I was starting to get overly stressed about everything, so she said to me, "Mom, you need to take a walk!"

It's that simple . . . take a walk. In the past I allowed the fallout from loss to dictate my overall well-being and, unfortunately, my relationship with the Lord and those I love. However, I have learned to respond rather than react. In doing so, my personal workout time has become a vital routine that has changed the trajectory of my life. It has helped me process and navigate through deep-seated emotional pain and heartbreak as well as grow close to the Lord again. First Timothy 4:8 tells us,

> Physical training is of some value, but godliness has value for all things, holding promise for both the present life and the life to come.

Due to the intensity of my circumstances, physical training brought me back to a life of godliness, which is valuable for both this present life and the life to come.

If you are struggling with a severe loss, prayer and Bible study will no doubt be the most noteworthy and life-changing tools in helping you find true peace and authentic joy. However, as "unspiritual" as working up a good sweat may sound, in my experience, exercising proved that the Word of God is true: "Physical training is of some value."

Peace in the face of loss comes when you **honor God with your body** through a good workout and let exercise renew your perspective and emotions.

35

Gracious words are a honeycomb,
sweet to the soul and healing to the bones.

PROVERBS 16:24

WHILE JIM WAS IN A NEW YORK CITY HOSPITAL going through chemotherapy and radiation treatments, Camryn, Erin, and I agreed that the city view outside his room might work in the movies, but it was definitely not helpful for healing. Neither was the interior, which was a typical hospital room—stark white and gray, dreary and dull. So we decided to brighten up the place with words. Words that would inspire hope. Words filled with truth. Words that Jim and everyone else who walked into the room would see, believe, and (we hoped) repeat. The girls and I went to work with drawing paper, colored markers, and the Bible, and we tried to be as creative and colorful as possible. We posted words of encouragement and life everywhere around the dreary hospital room, including on Jim's tray table and the television hanging in the corner. Wherever there was empty space, we filled it.

After six weary weeks in New York City, Jim was transferred to a hospital in Buffalo where he would complete the remainder of his cancer treatment protocol. When we arrived, we unpacked the "reminder signs" and posted them on the hospital-room walls where Jim could see them.

Once Jim and his doctors felt that he was well enough to leave the hospital, we packed his bags again, took down all the reminder signs, and—finally—went home.

Unfortunately, not all the signs survived the packing and unpacking. However, the ones that did are posted on the bathroom mirror in front of Jim's sink even now! Although tattered, torn, and taped on all sides, those words continue to remind our family of the truth every day. Here are some of the messages:

- *Jesus has all authority over cancer. Therefore, cancer has no power.*
- *In Jesus' name, cancer leave my body.*
- *Jim, I will fight for you. You are mine!*
- *Jim, I will restore health to you, and heal you of your wounds—Jeremiah 30:17.*
- *Jim, I have given you power, love, and a sound mind! You can do this!*
- *Lord, I believe You can heal me. Forgive me for my unbelief.*

- *By JESUS' stripes, I AM HEALED!*
- *Your will, God, not mine be done!*
- *I am with you, Jim!*
- *I choose LIFE!*

🍃 🍃 🍃

As you go through this season of loss, what reminder messages do you need to create for yourself? What words of life do you need to start speaking so that your mind and heart can receive truth and live it? If you were to ask my daughters what I say to them almost as often as "I love you," they would share two words: *"Speak life!"* Life-giving words are those that fill the heart, mind, and soul with peace, truth, and life. I'm referring to words that have the power to change a person and the trajectory of his or her life even while circumstances do not change. *God's* words. These words are important anytime, but they are critical when we're dealing with loss or crisis. The moments when we're most discouraged and our perspective is skewed by pain are the moments when we most need to hear life-giving truth and be reminded of who God is.

If you need further inspiration regarding the importance of life-giving words, read some of the many reminders in the Bible. Here are just a few:

> The tongue has the power of life and death,
>   and those who love it will eat its fruit.

PROVERBS 18:21

This is convicting for me. Ponder for a moment how often you speak negative or discouraging words to yourself or others. The words you say have the power to give life or death—and if your words are not bringing life, what are they bringing? I read this quote by an unknown author not too long ago: "Words are free. It's how you use them that may cost you." Ouch. If this does not motivate us to choose our words wisely, I do not know what will.

Your word is a lamp to my feet
 and a light to my path.
PSALM 119:105, ESV

God's Word is our life map or, better put, our Basic Instructions Before Leaving Earth. Life is full of twists and turns, mountains and valleys, yet our gracious, kind, loving God does not expect us just to wing it on our own. No, He has provided "everything we need for life and godliness" through His Word and Spirit (see 2 Peter 1:3). We have everything we need; we just need to access and apply it. You cannot speak life if you do not know words that give life. And you cannot know life-giving words if you do not know the Giver of Life through His Word.

Whatever you do, whether in word or deed, do it all in the name of the Lord Jesus, giving thanks to God the Father through him.
COLOSSIANS 3:17

A common cliché tells us that our actions speak louder than our words. And while that might be true most of the time, the words we speak have the power to dictate our actions. If you remember whom you're living for, you will be more mindful of the words you speak and the actions that result. They work together, hand in hand.

My daughters have their own reminder messages of life-giving words. Camryn's are written in black marker on the mirror fastened to the back of her bedroom door:

- *Don't take anything for granted!*
- *Never Give Up!*
- *I am fearfully and wonderfully made.*
- *Everything happens for a reason!*
- *Be Strong!*
- *Trust in God!*
- *Jesus Loves Me!*
- *Everything is going to be okay!*

Erin Marie's life messages are posted on the inside of her closet door:

- *My God is SOVEREIGN over all things.*
- *You make me BRAVE.*
- *Jesus, only YOU can be King of my heart. I surrender all to YOU!*
- *Life is short . . . LIVE!!!*
- *There is power in the Name of Jesus!*

• *Heavenly Father . . . my prayer is not that you would remove the struggle . . . but that You would give me more of Yourself in the midst of it.*

I just realized that I do not have a single reminder message of my own posted anywhere. It's time that you and I get busy writing some life-giving realities down on paper. When we're dealing with pain, when we're wrestling with God's plan, when our loss consumes us and life seems overwhelming—these are times when we need to speak *life*, to ourselves and others. As Erin's reminder said, "Life is short . . . LIVE." And living becomes a lot more joyful and peace filled when we are mindful of the words we meditate on and the words we speak.

I think it is vital that God have the last word here—and this is really a prayer as well:

> May the words of my mouth and the meditation of
> my heart
> be pleasing in your sight,
> O LORD, my Rock and my Redeemer.

PSALM 19:14

Peace in the midst of loss can be found
when we **choose to speak life**.

210

36

When my father and my mother forsake me,
then the LORD will take care of me.

PSALM 27:10, NKJV

WE ALL HAVE OUR SHARE of heartbreaking stories and the emotional scars that remain as a result. And yet, with every heartbreaking circumstance and every tear, God's faithfulness stands firm and steadfast. No matter what we lose, we will never lose the faithfulness of God—regardless of how dark our surroundings are.

It's one thing to talk about God's faithfulness after a crisis has passed, when we've started to heal emotionally and we can look back and see—even through our tears—how God was present in our pain. It's something else altogether to be convinced of God's faithfulness when we're still in the middle of the trial. When we don't see an end in sight. When we can't think of anything worse than what we're going through. If that's what you're experiencing, my heart goes out to you and I encourage you to read on.

The story I want to share today is from a woman named Faith, a woman who dealt with unbearable heartbreak and yet clung to the truth of God's enduring faithfulness.

Faith and her husband, Dale, founded Speaking Truth in Love Ministries, an organization dedicated to helping churches, leaders, and ministries deal with the devastating aftermath of sexual abuse within Christian communities. Faith is a survivor of sexual abuse. Her wisdom and experience are well worth heeding, and I believe you will discover that there is much to be gained from her loss.

I'll let her share:

I was five years old when I came to accept Christ as my personal Lord and Savior. My father had presented the gospel message during Easter Sunday service, and I realized that I needed the forgiveness that Christ's sacrifice provided. Since that time I have not wavered in my faith.

While I grew up in a home that appeared to be the perfect pastor's family, nothing could have been further from the truth. Still, in spite of the dysfunction and hypocrisy, God remained my fortress and rock. And though I grew up in a family with two parents and eight brothers, I often felt completely alone, like I could not trust anyone. . . .

The reason for this inability to trust was that I had been abused by one of the most important people in my life, someone I should have been able to trust completely—my father. It all began when I was a vulnerable nine-year-old and continued until I was a senior in high school.

Because of my inability to trust, I remained silent most of the time. But I spoke to God often. I remember walking home from the school bus praying and singing praises to Him. I clung to verses like Psalm 28:6-7, "Praise be to the LORD, for he has heard my cry for mercy. The LORD is my strength and my shield; my heart trusts in him, and I am helped. My heart leaps for joy and I will give thanks to him in song."

When the abuse started I died emotionally. I believe God gives us these coping mechanisms in order to survive until we are emotionally, spiritually, psychologically, and physically ready to deal with the abuse. The numbing effect of shutting down emotionally allows you to be able to function without being overcome with anger, bitterness, and depression. I built walls around my heart and was very selective in sharing with anyone. And yet, despite all that was torn away, by His grace I ultimately became a patchwork of hope and healing woven together by God's love and faithfulness.

Even though I experienced God's peace through the years of abuse, my true healing journey began

when God opened up the deep wounds in my
heart where my emotions had been lying dormant.
"He reached down from on high and took hold
of me; he drew me out of deep waters. He rescued
me from my powerful enemy, from my foes, who
were too strong for me. They confronted me in the
day of my disaster, but the LORD was my support"
(Psalm 18:16-18).

During this time, God called me, along with
my husband, to start a ministry to help those
dealing with abuse and domestic violence. He
revealed this great need to us, and the ministry
continues to thrive and bring peace and comfort to
me and countless others.

Don't you admire Faith's *faith*? After being defiled for
nine agonizing years, she still trusted God one day at a time
and didn't succumb to bitterness, anger, vengeance, or even
the ache to be validated. She focused on God's love, His
goodness, and the truth found in His Word.

Because this fallen world is riddled with sin and blinded
by spiritual darkness, we are all often on the wrong end
of abuse in one way or another. We can all relate to being
victimized or routinely let down by others in so many ways.
You may not have endured the intense abuse that Faith
did, but maybe you have endured a boss who misused his
authority to make your life miserable . . . a fair-weather
friend who took a shot at you below the belt because he or

she was jealous . . . a cruel Facebook post or Twitter tweet directed at you. We've all been there in one way or another.

And then there are the really hard-core hits, such as horrible bullying on social media, being lied to and ripped off by those we believe in, or being burned in a romantic relationship. Maybe you, like Faith, have suffered loss at the hands of someone who was supposed to love and protect you. Maybe you have died emotionally and built walls around your heart. I cannot even begin to understand your journey or how deep your pain is. But there is a God who sees and knows and has proclaimed over and over again in His Word that He is a faithful, ever-present God who rescues, saves, and turns our darkness into light. The answer is the same no matter how different the hurt and heartbreak are: "You, O Lord, keep my lamp burning; my God turns my darkness into light" (Psalm 18:28).

Jerry Bridges writes eloquently about the way God can use our pain: "God's infinite wisdom then is displayed in bringing good out of evil, beauty out of ashes. It is displayed in turning all the forces of evil that rage against His children into good for them. But the good that He brings about is often different from the good we envision."[13] In the end, Faith allowed the Lord to use her deep pain and loss for good—so that through her ministry she might be able to comfort others with the comfort that God has given her. Faith has said that Psalm 27 is very significant to her and holds special meaning and hope for anyone facing abuse. I'd like to leave you with a passage that she often turned to:

I would have lost heart, unless I had believed
That I would see the goodness of the LORD
In the land of the living.

Wait on the LORD;
Be of good courage,
And He shall strengthen your heart;
Wait, I say, on the LORD!

PSALM 27:13-14, NKJV

Peace in the depths of loss can be found when
you trust and believe that you will eventually
experience God's goodness.

37

The best way out is always through.

ROBERT FROST

"No matter how bad things become, there's always light at the end of the tunnel. As long as you have faith in God and love for each other, you can make it — no matter what."

Those are the words of Marlies, a friend of a friend who graciously shared her triumph through loss and tragedy with me, and now with you. Her family's story takes place before I was born, during Hitler's reign of terror in the late 1930s and early 1940s.

Marlies was born not far from where I live, in a little town called Naples, New York, and was raised in the throes of the Great Depression. At the tender age of four, she and her pregnant mother, her father, and her brother boarded the ocean liner *Bremen* to cross the Atlantic Ocean and visit her cancer-stricken grandfather in Germany. What Marlies's parents planned as a three-month stay ended up a seven-year nightmare.

At first, things got off to a great start as they settled into a comfortable routine on her grandparents' farm. But the cozy serenity of farm life was shattered as the shadows of World War II fell across the land. The borders were closed, and the family was trapped. The happy reunion became overshadowed by the burden of survival as the family began to starve under the iron fist of Nazi rule. They endured things most of us only read about in history books, from air raids and assaults to intimidation tactics by the Gestapo, and finally Marlies was sent away to live with a relative. You have probably read stories and watched documentaries of World War II, but can you fathom living through it? Would your faith in God's goodness and faithfulness waver? Would you grow bitter and resentful? What a test of faith and perseverance this family had to endure.

As if the story could get any more hellish, the relative Marlies was sent to live with was abusive, treating her like a slave rather than a family member. It wasn't bad enough to endure the horrors of war, starvation, suffering, and life as a stranger in a strange land; she had to withstand appalling abuse on top of everything else.

She was finally brought back to her grandparents' farm, but for seven long, ugly years she experienced atrocities and prejudices through a hostile school, bombing raids, and Nazi persecution. It was as if she took a guided tour through the valley of the shadow of death, seeing it all through the eyes of a child grappling with an adult world. Young Marlies struggled to make sense of the senseless horrors, but, astonishingly, she remained undaunted.

Even after the war, she and her family were often marginalized and rejected by the occupying Allies, even though they were American citizens. Getting home was no easy task, but in time and by God's grace they made their way back to the United States.

In the end, Marlies, her mother, father, and now two brothers were restored to a life filled with love for God and each other. The war was horrendous, but their faith, although tested, proved resilient and steadfast. They never lost sight of God's promises or gave up on His faithfulness.

🍂 🍂 🍂

Marlies's experience makes me think of the remarkable story of Jesus walking on water in the midst of a fierce storm:

> When the disciples saw him walking on the lake, they were terrified. "It's a ghost," they said, and cried out in fear.
>
> But Jesus immediately said to them: "Take courage! It is I. Don't be afraid."
>
> "Lord, if it's you," Peter replied, "tell me to come to you on the water."
>
> "Come," he said.
>
> Then Peter got down out of the boat, walked on the water and came toward Jesus. But when

he saw the wind, he was afraid and, beginning to
sink, cried out, "Lord, save me!" Immediately Jesus
reached out his hand and caught him.

MATTHEW 14:26-31

My heart resonates with Peter in so many ways. Does
yours? The apostle Peter spent three years with Jesus. I cannot
imagine even spending three minutes with Jesus. They ate
together, prayed together, did life together. Peter witnessed
the miracles—Jesus turning water into wine, raising Lazarus
from the dead, healing the sick, casting out demons . . . Peter
was there for all of it. Yet at times his faith still faltered.

And that is what I appreciate so much in this story—
Peter's authenticity. He was afraid and he was not ashamed.
He could have postured and acted all cool when he was
sinking in the water because his friends were there watching, including Jesus. And that's the thing: People are watching when we struggle. They don't pay attention when life
is rolling along beautifully—no, people pay close attention
when life is falling apart because they want to see whether
what we say we believe in is actually true. People want to
know whether the fire of adversity will burn us or make us
radiate God's glory all the more.

So Peter's faith faltered, and he began to sink. But he
didn't go under because he knew that Jesus was there, and
he called out to Him. What does this teach us? Without
a doubt, our faith will be tested. However, it is not about
whether our faith falters in those moments but what we do

in response to the testing. Peter called out to Jesus. You and I can do the same.

My favorite part of this entire story is Jesus' response when Peter calls out to him: "Immediately Jesus reached out his hand." *Immediately*. Jesus did not wait until Peter was under water, gasping for air, drowning. As soon as Peter called out for help, Jesus responded. And I believe that is exactly what He will do for us. We might not see the results of His rescue plan, but that doesn't mean that He does not immediately reach out His hand to catch us before we hit rock bottom.

During the long storm Marlies and her family weathered in Nazi Germany, I imagine they had days when their faith faltered. Days when the violence jerked their focus away from the Lord. We have days like that too. But the Lord is and always will be greater than the storm. He is greater than what we see all around us, greater than the distractions and fears within us, and He knows how and when to intervene so that we can refocus on His greatness and power. His plan is always to lead us back home—back to Himself, where there is safety and peace beyond understanding. When we call on Him, He will answer.

Peace in the storms of loss can be found when we **call out to Jesus** and trust Him to respond.

38

Sometimes your circle decreases in size
but increases in value.

UNKNOWN

DURING THE EARLY 1990s and at the height of my husband's celebrated football career—the four consecutive years the Bills played in the Super Bowl—we had a ton of "friends." I use quotation marks because most of the people who were around during that renowned season were not true friends. Unfortunately, we discovered this after Jim retired, the parties ceased, and our only son was diagnosed with a terminal disease.

Maybe you can relate. Before your life took a sharp detour, your friends were there for you, but now that the bottom has fallen out from beneath you, they are nowhere to be found. Because I know how painful this is, I hope and pray that you have not had to experience what we did. And yet, as a result of losing certain friends—or those whom Jim and I *thought* were friends—we have gained so much more than we ever lost.

Yes, some friendships come and go—sometimes for the right reasons and sometimes for the wrong ones. We all experience this. Maybe you are blessed to still have the same core group of friends today that you had in high school or college. Or maybe the friends that you used to have are gone because you ended up finding out exactly who your true friends were when your life fell apart. While it is a blessing to find out who your real friends are, it hurts when the people you thought would be there for you suddenly disappear when the roof caves in.

After Hunter was diagnosed, Jim and I were shattered. Initially, we were in a fog of denial and shock, trying to figure out how to cope with what would become our new normal. After the dust settled and life with a terminally ill child continued, the pain of our extended losses began to set in. Where did everyone go? What happened to all our so-called friends?

I had expected certain people, both friends and family members, to be there for us during our darkest hours. When they were nowhere to be found, my disappointment and frustration unleashed anger and resentment that festered for years. Thinking about it makes me so sad, and I wish I'd known then what I know now. Even though I did not realize it at the time, God was at work in the midst of it all, revealing His grace and love to our family in ever-increasing measure.

What we had considered loss at the time ended up being the hand of God graciously paving the way for us to find new, vibrant relationships. We discovered friendships that were birthed in the season of our greatest need, affliction, and heartache. Our loss ended up leading to relationships that we would not have today if it were not for the ones that were taken away. People who have wept with us, prayed for us, loved us unconditionally, and blessed us beyond measure. People who live Proverbs 17:17, "A friend loves at all times."

Some days, when I was exhausted and sad, I would go to the mailbox to find a card filled with encouragement. Or I would receive a phone call from someone who felt led to pray with me just when I needed it most. Our new friends not only covered us in prayer, they made time for us, ran to the grocery store when we couldn't, and found ways to do what needed to be done because we had no time to do anything but take care of Hunter.

When I think about the people that God brought into our lives, I cannot help but think about what Jesus said in the Gospel of John:

My command is this: Love each other as I have loved you. Greater love has no one than this, that he lay down his life for his friends.

JOHN 15:12-13

How do we love each other the way Jesus loves us? And what does it mean to lay down our lives? Jesus was the perfect example of both love and sacrifice. If His love dwells in me, then I have everything I need to extend to others the kind of unconditional love Jesus is referring to. He loved humankind so much that He willingly gave His life so that we could experience His love and freely give it to others. And it wasn't only at the Cross. He also poured out His love while He walked the earth—He laid down His life daily for the good of others.

I'm sure you're familiar with the verse that proclaims this truth about Jesus: "For God so loved the world that he gave his one and only Son, that whoever believes in him shall not perish but have eternal life" (John 3:16). Whenever I read this amazing verse, I remind myself of this: If God took care of my eternity through Jesus, He will take care of my today and all my tomorrows (including every detail of every relationship) until I see Him face-to-face in heaven.

Would you be willing to consider that sometimes God's blessings are not in what He gives but in what He takes away? Are you open to the possibility that maybe He has removed a relationship or friendship from your life for your own protection and good? I appreciate what Graham Cooke said: "[God] allows in His wisdom what He could easily prevent by His power."[14] It is not only God's wisdom and power but also His perfect love that orchestrates the details of our lives, including our relationships. Can you trust that God sovereignly intervenes so that you have the people in your life right now that He wants to be there for you?

"It is comforting to know that everything God sends

is the best possible thing for [us]. Nothing can derail his plan."[15] Vaneetha Rendall Risner's words are encouraging. Although you might not understand why God has allowed certain friendships to remain, others to end, and new ones to form, you can choose to trust that His plan is always intended to bring about the best possible outcome for everyone involved.

The important thing is that God, in His love, is weaving all our lives together in an eternal tapestry where each of us—current friends, former friends, and friends yet to come—is a part of something inconceivably beautiful.

> Peace in the face of loss comes when we **trust God** to bring into our lives the relationships He has chosen for us.

39

I have heard your prayer and seen your tears;
I will heal you.

2 KINGS 20:5

MY MOTHER MEANS MORE to me than words could ever express. She is my best friend and confidante; she's an endless source of wisdom, commonsense advice, encouragement, and accountability; and her unconditional love for me is limitless. God has used her more than any other person to influence my relationship with Him.

My mom was caring for Hunter when he took his last breath on earth. She shared his final evening and had the privilege of tucking him in for the last time as he slipped from our world into eternity. His final night—and her journey of learning to trust God's perfect timing—is a poignant, heartrending story that I have asked her to share with you:

They say time heals all wounds, but maybe
God chooses to use time to heal—physically,

emotionally, and spiritually. For He alone is the
healer, not time. Time is a tool, just as a paintbrush
is a tool in the hand of an artist or a pen in the
hand of the poet.

On August 4, 2005, Hunter was staying at my
house for the night. He had had a great day filled
with lots of fun activities—but something was
different. Hunter was unusually quiet and had an
extraordinary peace about him.

I remember him staring at me as I held him
in the Jacuzzi for his daily water therapy. I was
so struck by the way he was looking at me that
I called for the nurse to come in and see it for
herself. I had never seen him peer into me like that
before. I held him and gazed back, treasuring the
moment.

Then, as always, I said to him, "Hey, you, my
Best Boy in the whole world. I love you, buddy."
I followed up with our favorite song, "Soldier Boy."

Hunter truly was a soldier, battling bravely on
the front lines of the fight of his life each day.

It was well after midnight when Jill had left
to go home for the night and Hunter was in bed,
sound asleep. All was quiet and peaceful when I
finally dozed off next to him. I don't know how
long we'd been sleeping when suddenly I awoke
and noticed that Hunter was not breathing.
Immediately I began doing everything I knew to

help Hunter, everything that had always worked in the past to get him to breathe again.

My husband, Jerry, was sleeping in a room at the other end of the house. I kept screaming, hoping that eventually he would hear me calling for help. He never responded, so I had to leave Hunter and run down the hall to wake him up. That moment was like a nightmare. Screaming at the top of my lungs with no one hearing me. I needed Jerry; I needed him to call 911; I needed help . . .

Jerry called 911 and Jill while I continued to do whatever I could to help Hunter. A group of EMTs arrived within minutes, and they began trying to revive Hunter as they put him in the ambulance. I sat in the front by the driver, and, oddly, the first thing I noticed was the clock and the numbers 5:55. The rest of what happened that morning once we arrived at the hospital is somewhat of a blur, and I suppose that's a good thing.

Hunter went to heaven that morning. For years after that day, every time I saw 5:00, 5:50, or 5:55 on the clock, my heart would feel the horror of that morning: the panic and utter helplessness, the horror of death. I prayed desperately for years that I would no longer wake up feeling this way.

Then one morning, ten years later, I woke up with my eyes fixed on the clock, and there it was again, as on so many mornings before: 5:55. But curiously, this time was not like all the others. This time my heart was filled with overwhelming joy. God in His perfect timing had finally opened my eyes to the truth that I had been unable to see until now: that on August 5, 2005, at 5:55 a.m., He healed Hunter and brought him to heaven in a triumphant homecoming.

The horror of Hunter's death is gone and has been replaced by joy. After ten years of crying out to God to take away that horrible sense of dread and heal my wounded heart, He did. Why did it take ten years? I don't know. But what I do know is that I trust Him and His timing.

They say time heals all wounds. No. It is God who heals in His perfect time.

I love my mother. Her honesty, vulnerability, and trust in God encourage, comfort, and challenge me. I wish I had been with Hunter that night, but in God's wisdom and perfect plan, it was not to be. That gift was given to my mom, and until she penned this piece for the devotional, she had never shared her struggle with me.

Maybe, like my mom, you have been traumatized by unexpected and devastating circumstances beyond your control. Maybe, like her, you have been struggling with the emotional aftershocks of what happened to you for days, months, or even years. Have you taken to avoiding the radio because you might hear a song that reminds you of the one you loved and lost? Is there a special place you cannot bring yourself to drive by because just seeing it shreds you emotionally? Could it be that a specific time on the clock brings back waves of anguish?

If there are reminders you have been avoiding, running from, and afraid of, or that you just cannot bring yourself to deal with because of the deep hurt in your soul—my friend, take heart! Jesus is still Lord over all. In His perfect timing, in His perfect way, your healing, peace, and wholeness will come—just as Hunter's did and just as my mother's did.

The book of Ecclesiastes tells us,

> There is a time for everything,
>   and a season for every activity under the heavens:
>
> a time to be born and a time to die. . . .
>
> He has made everything beautiful in its time. He has also set eternity in the human heart; yet no one can fathom what God has done from beginning to end.
>
> ECCLESIASTES 3:1-2, 11

Furthermore, regardless of how our circumstances might make it appear, God has not fallen off His throne. He is still presiding over history, and His will shall still be done on earth as it is in heaven. Nothing comes as a surprise to Him. He's calling the shots and crafting the outcomes until He comes! He is working right now, in the midst of every single detail in your life.

Timing is never wasted in His Kingdom. He is using this time to cultivate your character. He is completing the good work He started in you. And no matter how you feel in this moment, the emotions and circumstances surrounding your life are for your good.

God's timing, decision-making processes, and values are not based on earthly standards and goals. His ways and timing are perfect! He is never early and never late, but always right on time.

> Peace in the face of loss comes when we **trust that God's timing for healing is perfect**.

No God; no peace. Know God; know peace.

UNKNOWN

OF ALL THE MESSAGES I have shared with you, this one is by far the most important. When I began my search for God and truth, eight months after Hunter was diagnosed, I was crushed in spirit, desperate for hope, and filled with fear and despair. I did not have time or room in my heart for mere religion. I longed for a faith that was real and a God who was faithful—and that is exactly what I found.

As a result of my search, I found the gospel message and the Jesus that it declares. Both are as vital to life as the oxygen that fills my lungs. I came to understand that the Bible is not just an ancient historical book chronicling the antiquity of humankind, but an intimate love story written by our Creator, through the pen of humans, to the broken heart of the sinner.

My uncle Mark was the first person to share the gospel story with me—the story of our sinful nature, our need for a Savior, and God's amazing love displayed through the life, death, and resurrection of Jesus. Of all the things that Mark said during our many visits together, there's one thing I will never forget as long as I live. He looked at me and said passionately, "Jill, as much as you love your children, you will never know what real love is until you know the love of God through His Son, Jesus."

Initially I was offended because I could not fully comprehend a love greater than a mother's love for her children. Still, I was intrigued and wanted the love that Uncle Mark talked about. The Bible says,

> Dear friends, let us love one another, for love comes from God. Everyone who loves has been born of God and knows God. Whoever does not love does not know God, because God is love. This is how God showed his love among us: He sent his one and only Son into the world that we might live through him. This is love: not that we loved God, but that he loved us and sent his Son as an atoning sacrifice for our sins.
>
> 1 JOHN 4:7-10

Love comes from God because He is love. If you want to experience authentic, unconditional love, you need to know God. The Bible also identifies God as the God of peace (see

1 Thessalonians 5:23). Therefore, if you know God, you can experience real, abiding peace. Not the kind of peace the world offers, which is really just the absence of conflict, but the kind that our heavenly Father offers to His children, the kind the Bible describes as "peace . . . which transcends all understanding, [that] will guard your hearts and your minds in Christ Jesus" (Philippians 4:7).

Some of you may have already embraced the gospel. But some of you might be wondering exactly what the gospel message is and how to know the love and peace of God. Your heart may be aching with that epic question "How can I have a relationship with God?" Jesus was pretty clear: It's all about relationship, not religion! "Jesus answered, 'I am the way and the truth and the life. No one comes to the Father except through me'" (John 14:6).

Look at the state of the human heart as described in Romans 3:23: *"All have sinned and fall short of the glory of God."* Although we often fail to acknowledge it, sin has serious consequences, which we see in Romans 6:23: *"The wages of sin is death."* Death has infested and devoured the earth. Every one of us has a limited shelf life, but even worse is that we are spiritually dead within. And because of that, even our best efforts fail. You cannot fill an eternal soul with anything from this world. However, the good news is that God loves us too much to leave us stranded, so He made a way for us to reach Him. The second part of Romans 6:23 points to our hope: *"But the gift of God is eternal life in Christ Jesus our Lord."*

Romans 5:8 describes the extent of God's love. He doesn't wait for us to clean up our act because He knows that we can't. *"God demonstrates His own love for us, in that while we were yet sinners, Christ died for us"* (NASB). Amazing! Christ went to the cross on our behalf while we were His enemies. Knowing all this, how should we respond? The answer is found in Romans 10:13: *"Whoever will call on the name of the Lord will be saved"* (NASB). A relationship with God is not found in church, Bible study, theology, or good deeds—though there's a place for all of that. It is found in calling on the name of the Lord in childlike faith.

The process is illuminated in Romans 10:9-10: *"If you confess with your mouth Jesus as Lord, and believe in your heart that God raised Him from the dead, you will be saved; for with the heart a person believes, resulting in righteousness, and with the mouth he confesses, resulting in salvation"* (NASB).

Finally, through this process there is an exchange of lives. We surrender ours to Jesus, and Jesus gives us His life—He comes to live within us. Mark 8:34 tells us, *"Then he called the crowd to him along with his disciples and said: 'Whoever wants to be my disciple must deny themselves and take up their cross and follow me.'"* This world is filled with many crosses, and we all have ours to bear. But as we follow Him, the peace, hope, and love we ache for is ours because He who is love now lives in us.

Regardless of how great your loss, how deep your heartbreak, or how dire your circumstances right now, if you know Jesus, you can know and experience peace—no matter what.

First Peter 3:15 tells us, "Always be prepared to give an answer to everyone who asks you to give the reason for the hope that you have." So here is the reason for the hope, joy, and peace that you and I have despite the heartbreaking losses we have suffered and endured: Jesus.

He is the reason.

He is the answer.

He is PEACE!

Without Him we have nothing, including the peace we desperately need.

With Him we have everything.

He is everything

Now in Christ Jesus you who once were far away have been brought near by the blood of Christ. For he himself is our peace.

EPHESIANS 2:13-14

Now may the Lord of peace himself give you peace at all times and in every way. The Lord be with all of you.

2 THESSALONIANS 3:16

Peace in the face of loss comes when you know and **trust the Prince of Peace**.

ACKNOWLEDGMENTS

A book like this would not be possible without the providence and grace of God. Therefore, first and foremost I would like to thank Him . . . for His Son, Jesus, and for His relentless love, compassion, and comfort. We are able to know and experience peace in the face of loss because of the Prince of Peace. Thank YOU, Jesus.

For the *Tyndale Team*—Sarah Atkinson, Sharon Leavitt, Jillian Schlossberg, and Karin Buursma. Working with all of you has been a blessing beyond measure. Thank you for inviting me in and making me feel at home. It has been an honor and a privilege. I pray that God will bless all of you immeasurably more than you could ever ask or imagine.

For *Jana Burson*—my friend, literary agent, and fellow football lover. Once again, God has allowed us to be a part of something greater, far beyond our ability to comprehend. So grateful for you!

For *Rick Kern*—After all these years, we're still going strong, still seeking the heart of God, still trusting and believing, still editing and praying and writing and praying more. Can't do this without you, Rick. Thank you.

For *my family*—Jim, Erin, Cam, Mom, and Dad. Thank you for praying me through once again. I love you so much and thank God for allowing me to do life with all of you.

> *But if I say, "I will not mention his word*
> *or speak anymore in his name,"*
> *his word is in my heart like a fire,*
> *a fire shut up in my bones.*
> *I am weary of holding it in;*
> *indeed, I cannot.*
> JEREMIAH 20:9

ENDNOTES

1. Elisabeth Elliot, *Passion and Purity: Learning to Bring Your Love Life under Christ's Control* (Grand Rapids, MI: Revell, 2006), 163–164.
2. Erin Kelly with Jill Kelly, *Kelly Tough: Live Courageously by Faith* (Racine, WI: BroadStreet, 2015), 180.
3. Adapted from Jill Kelly, *Without a Word: How a Boy's Unspoken Love Changed Everything* (New York: FaithWords, 2010), 183–184.
4. Erin Kelly with Jill Kelly, *Kelly Tough: Live Courageously by Faith* (Racine, WI: Broadstreet, 2015), 192–194.
5. Elisabeth Elliot, *Shadow of the Almighty: The Life and Testament of Jim Elliot* (New York: HarperCollins, 1958), 91.
6. Morgan Matson, *Second Chance Summer* (New York: Simon and Schuster, 2013), 368.
7. Quoted in Elisabeth Elliot, *Through Gates of Splendor* (Carol Stream, IL: Tyndale, 1981), 20.
8. "Understanding MRSA Infection—the Basics," WebMD website, accessed September 13, 2016, http://www.webmd.com/skin-problems-and-treatments /understanding-mrsa#1.
9. A. W. Tozer, *The Knowledge of the Holy* (New York: HarperCollins, 1961), 53.
10. Billy Graham, *The Journey: How to Live by Faith in an Uncertain World* (Nashville: W Publishing Group, 2006), 68.
11. Adapted from Jill Kelly, *Without a Word: How a Boy's Unspoken Love Changed Everything*, 172–173, 177.
12. Mayo Clinic Staff, "Depression and Anxiety: Exercise Eases Symptoms," Mayo Clinic website, accessed August 31, 2016, http://www.mayoclinic.org /diseases-conditions/depression/in-depth/depression-and-exercise/art -20046495.
13. Jerry Bridges, *Trusting God: Even When Life Hurts* (Colorado Springs: NavPress, 2008), 128.
14. Graham Cooke, *A Divine Confrontation* (Shippensburg, PA: Destiny Image, 1999), 326.
15. Vaneetha Rendall Risner, "Is My Suffering Meaningless?" *Desiring God* (blog), July 12, 2014, http://www.desiringgod.org/articles/is-my-suffering -meaningless.

For more information about the
Hunter's Hope Foundation, please visit
www.HuntersHope.org.

"For I know the plans I have for you," says the LORD.
"They are plans for good and not for disaster,
to give you a future and a hope."

JEREMIAH 29:11, NLT

ABOUT THE AUTHOR

JILL KELLY is the wife of former Buffalo Bills quarterback and NFL Hall of Famer Jim Kelly and the mother of three. Jim and Jill's middle child and only son, Hunter, was diagnosed with Krabbe leukodystrophy, a fatal disease, as an infant. In September 1997, three months after his diagnosis, Jim and Jill established the Hunter's Hope Foundation. As chairman of the board, Jill helps families affected by leukodystrophy through the foundation's work to raise awareness and research funds to fight these diseases.

A celebrated author, Jill has written or collaborated on several books, including *Without a Word* and *Kelly Tough*, both *New York Times* bestsellers. She is also a sought-after public speaker. Jill and Jim live in the Buffalo area with their two daughters and four dogs.

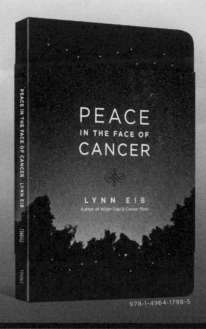